P9-DJL-215

ALSO BY DONALD J. TRUMP

Trump: The Art of the Deal
Trump: Surviving at the Top
Trump: The Art of the Comeback
The America We Deserve
Trump: How to Get Rich

TRUMP
Think Like a Billionaire

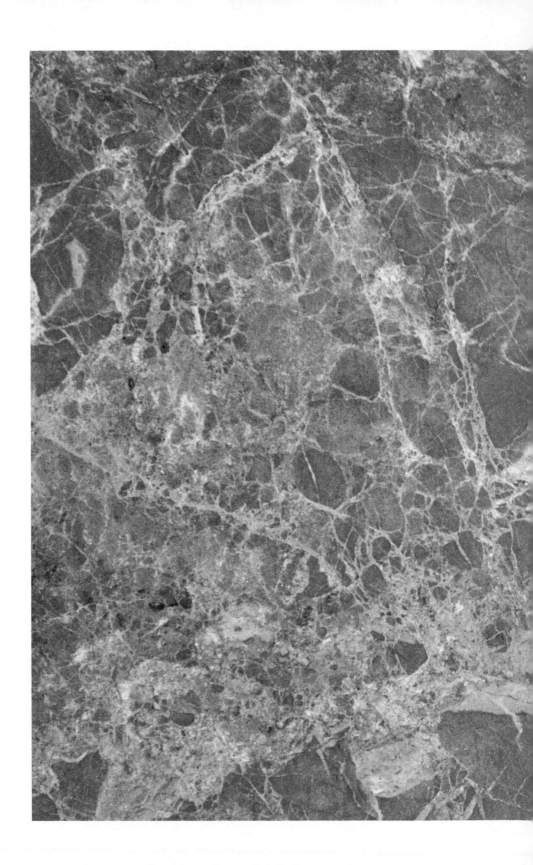

TRUMP

Think Like a Billionaire

Everything You Need to Know
About Success, Real Estate,
and Life

Donald J. Trump

with Meredith McIver

RANDOM HOUSE
NEW YORK

Copyright © 2004 by Donald J. Trump

All rights reserved under International and Pan-American Copyright
Conventions. Published in the United States by Random House, an imprint
of The Random House Publishing Group, a division of Random House, Inc.,
New York, and simultaneously in Canada by Random House
of Canada Limited, Toronto.

RANDOM HOUSE and colophon are registered trademarks
of Random House, Inc.

Except where noted, all photos courtesy
of Donald J. Trump/The Trump Organization.

ISBN 1-4000-6355-8

Printed in the United States of America on acid-free paper
Random House website address: www.atrandom.com

2 4 6 8 9 7 5 3 1

FIRST EDITION

Book design by Carole Lowenstein

To my parents,
Mary and Fred Trump

The Father of All Advice

*"Know everything you can
about what you're doing."*
—MY FATHER, FRED TRUMP

*"In business everyone is out to grab, to fight,
to win. Either you are the under or the over dog.
It is up to you to be on top."*
—ALICE FOOTE MACDOUGALL

*"Being good in business is the most fascinating kind of art. . . .
Making money is art and working is art and
good business is the best art."*
—ANDY WARHOL

Contents

Introduction
Thinking Like a Billionaire

In a world of more than six billion people, there are only 587 billionaires. It's an exclusive club. Would you like to join us?

Of course, the odds against you are about ten million to one. But if you think like a billionaire, those odds shouldn't faze you at all.

Billionaires don't care what the odds are. We don't listen to common sense or do what's conventional or expected. We follow our vision, no matter how crazy or idiotic other people think it is. That's what this book is about—learning how to think like a billionaire. Even if you absorb only ten percent of the wisdom in this book, you'll still have a good shot at becoming a millionaire.

In my previous book, *How to Get Rich,* I shared some of my favorite techniques for running a profitable business and becoming a TV megastar. Consider this new book the second part of an ongoing conversation between you and The Donald—the billionaire's equivalent of those bestselling works of inspiration *Conversations with God* and *Conversations with God, Book 2.*

I'm sure some wise guy in the media is going to accuse me of comparing myself to God, so for the record, I do not think I am God.

I believe in God. If God ever wanted an apartment in Trump Tower, I would immediately offer my best luxury suite at a very special price. I believe God is everywhere and in all of us, and I want every decision I make to reflect well on me when it's time for me to go to that big boardroom in the sky. When I get permanently fired by the ultimate boss, I want the elevator to heaven to go up, not down.

Some of you may think it's wrong to talk about God and business in the same breath, but God has always been central to our way of thinking about capitalism. The Protestant work ethic has thrived for centuries. The pursuit of prosperity is ingrained in our religious culture. The more you have, the more you can give.

Here's something else about God that any billionaire knows: He's in the details, and you need to be there, too. I couldn't run a business any other way. When I'm talking to a contractor, or examining a site, or planning a new development, no detail is too small to consider. I even try to sign as many checks as possible. For me, there's nothing worse than a computer signing checks. When you sign a check yourself, you're seeing what's really going on inside your business, and if people see your signature at the bottom of the check, they know you're watching them, and they screw you less because they have proof that you care about the details.

I learned how to think like a billionaire by watching my father, Fred Trump. He was the greatest man I'll ever know, and the biggest influence on my life.

A lot has been written about my family. A writer named Gwenda Blair spent twelve years on her thorough history, *The Trumps: Three Generations That Built an Empire.* She even traced our lineage back to 1608, when a German lawyer named Hanns Drumpf settled in the town of Kallstadt, forty miles west of the Rhine River. According to Blair, one of my ancestors, a winegrower, changed the family name to

Trump at the end of the 1600s—a good move, I think, since Drumpf Tower doesn't sound nearly as catchy.

My grandfather Friedrich was the first Trump to come to America. Like many entrepreneurs, he ran away from home because he didn't want to work in the family wine business. One of my fellow billionaires, John R. Simplot, left his family farm because he didn't want to spend the rest of his days milking cows. Instead, he became a potato grower and one of the largest suppliers to McDonald's. He earned his billions in french fries. One way to think like a billionaire is to question your surroundings: Don't assume you have to accept the hand you were dealt.

My grandfather was a barber and the owner of several businesses, including a hotel and a restaurant. He moved from New York City to Seattle and eventually to Alaska during the gold rush, where he fed miners at the biggest joint in town, the Arctic Restaurant. Unfortunately, he caught pneumonia and died when my father was just a boy. My father never said much to me about him or about other Trump family history.

Fred C. Trump wasn't the kind of dad who took us to the movies or played catch with us in Central Park. He was better than those fathers. Instead, he'd take me to his building sites in Brooklyn and Queens. He'd say, "Let's make the rounds," and we'd be on our way. He never yelled at me or had to punish me, but he was always strong, and a little remote, until I joined his business. That's when I really got to know him.

I saw how he dealt with contractors and unions, and how he made the most out of every space. My father believed in adding "the extra element" to his properties—he was among the first to build garages into homes in Brooklyn. He could be a showman, too. His deals were front-page news in the Brooklyn newspapers. He advertised regularly and had big openings for his developments. His gift for promotion rubbed off on me, but it was never something we talked about, and to this day, I don't think promotion had much to do with either his success or mine. We succeeded because we learned how to create the best buildings at the best locations with the best zoning. My father showed me how to fight the unions and the politicians in order to get the building done under budget and ahead of schedule. And then, after the building is up and it's a great success, everyone says, "Boy, Donald, that was a great promotion," when promotion had nothing to do with it.

My father always trusted me. He'd been in business for fifty years, but he'd never let anyone else in the company sign his checks until I came to work. He had absolutely no doubt about my ability.

His faith gave me unshakable confidence. Even when I was at my lowest, in the early 1990s, when the real estate market tanked and I was billions in debt and Ivana and her lawyers and a hundred banks were ready to sue my ass off, my father told me he had absolutely no doubt that my business would be fine. He'd say, "You are a killer. You are a king."

My father never wanted to build in Manhattan. He thought it was too expensive. He'd say, "If I can buy a piece of land for a dollar a square foot in Brooklyn, why should I pay a thousand dollars a square foot in Manhattan?" It was a different philosophy, but it worked for him.

I'd been working in the family business for five years when I made the move into Manhattan. Some critics have suggested that my success is the result of family money, but family money didn't get my first Manhattan projects built. I had to raise tens of millions of dollars from investors for those jobs. It wasn't money that my father gave me; it was knowledge—knowledge that became instinctive for me.

When I was in college, I thought about becoming a movie producer, but whenever I talked to a friend about real estate, he would say, "Why would you want to make movies when you already know so much about real estate?" So yes, my father was a millionaire many times over, but if he hadn't shown me how to think about business, I never would have made it into the billionaires club.

I wish I could tell you that the billionaires club meets regularly at Mar-a-Lago, where we gather to analyze our portfolios, make blockbuster deals, eat caviar, and drink vintage wine, but the truth is: I don't drink, I'd rather eat a steak than caviar, and I've met only about twenty of the club members over the years, often on the golf course, where we tend to talk more about our game than our net worth. Still, I've studied fellow billionaires from afar, and I've also read what others have written about us.

In an article for *Forbes* by Matthew Herper, Robert Baron, a psychologist at Rensselaer Polytechnic Institute, said we are persuasive and have strong social skills—that we call upon our charisma to make a sale. In the same article, Kelly Shaver, a professor of psychology at William & Mary College, said we don't care what other people think about us. She said, "They're just happy to go off and do what they're doing."

I agree. My father thought I was nuts to build in Manhattan, but I didn't listen to him because I had my own vision. One of my favorite billionaires is Warren Buffett, who has his own vision, too. He didn't follow the stampede into the dot-com gold rush, even though he was widely criticized for remaining a traditional value investor. Now he once again looks like a genius. One of many things I admire about Warren is that in all of his years as CEO of Berkshire Hathaway, he has never sold one share of stock.

Another student of successful entrepreneurs, Michael Maccoby, a psychoanalyst and consultant, believes that billionaires like Jeff Bezos, Steve Jobs, and Ted Turner are successful in part because they are narcissists who devote their talent with unrelenting focus to achieving their dreams, even if it's sometimes at the expense of those around them. Maccoby's book *The Productive Narcissist* makes a convincing argument that narcissism can be a useful quality if you're trying to start a business. A narcissist does not hear the naysayers. At the Trump Organization, I listen to people, but my vision is my vision.

In *The Natural History of the Rich,* author Richard Conniff put it this way: "Almost all successful alpha personalities display a single-minded determination to impose their vision on the world, an irrational belief in unreasonable goals, bordering at times on lunacy." He quotes a passage from Michael Lewis on entrepreneur Jim Clark in *The New New Thing:* "He was the guy who always won the game of chicken because his opponents suspected he might actually enjoy a head-on collision." I doubt Jim Clark would enjoy that collision, but the fact that he has convinced people he might has a lot to do with his success.

Here are my top ten ways of thinking like a billionaire:

1. Don't take vacations. What's the point? If you're not enjoying your work, you're in the wrong job. Even when I'm playing golf, I'm doing business. I never stop, and I'm usually having fun. Now that my kids are joining the family business, I'm closer to them than I've ever been, and I'm finding out that I love relating to them just the way my father related to me—through a passion for work well done.

By the way, I'm not the only one who doesn't take vacations. My NBC compatriot Jay Leno works just as much as I do, and maybe that's one of the reasons he's stayed on top in the late-night ratings wars.

2. Have a short attention span. Most successful people have very short attention spans. It has a lot to do with imagination. Quite often, I'll be talking to someone and I'll know what they're going to say before they say it. After the first three words are out of their mouth, I can tell what the next forty are going to be, so I try to pick up the pace and move it along. You can get more done faster that way.

3. Don't sleep any more than you have to. I usually sleep about four hours per night. I'm in bed by 1 A.M. and up to read the newspapers at 5 A.M. That's all I need, and it gives me a competitive edge. I have friends who are successful and sleep ten hours a night, and I ask them, "How can you compete against people like me if I sleep only four hours?" It rarely can be done. No matter how brilliant you are, there's not enough time in the day.

You may be wondering: Why do you need a competitive edge? You don't, if you're happy to be an also-ran in life. In *The Natural History of the Rich,* Richard Conniff notes that it's common behavior for moguls to seek dominance. Even such traits as who makes the most eye contact in a conversation can be an indication of who seeks to dominate. Conniff singles me out as an example of someone who achieves dominance through my appearance, by leaving my eyebrows untrimmed in order to intimidate negotiating partners. I'm pleased to note that he doesn't comment on my hair.

4. Don't depend on technology. A lot of it is unnecessary and expensive. I don't have a computer on my desk. I don't use an intercom. When I want someone in my office, I yell. It works a lot better than an intercom, and it's much faster.

I don't even have an ATM card—I've never used one in my life. That's the funny thing about being rich: When I go to restaurants, I rarely have to pay. It's usually on the house. The sad part is that if I needed the money, they would make me pay!

I can understand why some people would appreciate the convenience of ATM cards, but a lot of other tech devices are completely unnecessary and get in the way of human contact. If you have something important to say, look the person in the eye and say it. And if you can't get there, pick up the phone and make sure they hear the sincerity in your voice. E-mail is for wimps.

5. Think of yourself as a one-man army. You're not only the commander in chief, you're the soldier as well. You must plan and execute your plan alone.

People are always comparing business to war and to sports. We do it because these are analogies we immediately understand, not because business is about toughness. It isn't. It's much more important to be smart than tough. I know some very bad businessmen who are brutally tough, but they're not smart people. They want to act like Vince Lombardi, but they don't know how to win. Lombardi would slap his players, even spit in their faces. He'd have three-hundred-pound men virtually crying. He could do that because he won, and you can do that only if you win.

Billionaires like to win. *The Natural History of the Rich* is full of examples of hypercompetitive plutocrats: Larry Ellison racing his yacht from Australia to Tasmania, Steve Fossett flying a balloon around the world, and Dennis Tito paying $20 million for a trip to space on a Russian rocket. "All of them, one way or another, were showing off," Conniff writes. "To put it in the biological context, they were engaging in display behavior. Animals do it all the time, and their displays, like ours, fall loosely into two categories: They show off with fine feathers, and they show off with risky behavior."

I have my own theory, but it's not as scientific: We do it because it's fun. Work hard, play hard, and live to the hilt.

6. It's often to your advantage to be underestimated. You never want people to think you're a loser or a schlepper, but it's not a good idea if they think you're the smartest guy in the room, either. Because I wrote *The Art of the Deal*, everyone is always on guard whenever I negotiate with them. One of the reasons President Reagan was such a successful candidate for office was because rival politicians consistently misjudged him. They assumed an actor wouldn't be able to compete. Through years of insults about his lack of intelligence and political

experience, Reagan would smile and remain genial, and in the end, he always exceeded expectations.

Because I'm too famous to be underestimated—I know that sounds egotistical, but it's true—I'm always impressed by ultrasuccessful people who live great lives in a low-key manner. For example, one of my neighbors in Trump Tower is a man named Joel Anderson. For years, I'd see him in the elevator and say hello, but I didn't know anything about him. One day he called my office and said, "Do you think it would be possible for Mr. Trump to attend my party?" He seemed like a nice guy, with a terrific wife, so I figured I'd pop in for a few minutes. When I got to the party, I was amazed to find myself surrounded by some of the most influential people in New York, including S. I. Newhouse and Anna Wintour. I soon discovered that mild-mannered Joel Anderson is the chairman and CEO of Anderson News, one of the country's largest distributors of newspapers and magazines. He's one of the most powerful and generous people I know. I'd been riding in the elevator with him for years and I never knew who he was.

In *How to Get Rich*, I discussed how important it is to let people know about your accomplishments. I'll always believe that, but there are times when it's even more impressive if people discover your accomplishments without you telling them directly. A few weeks after Joel Anderson's party, I noticed a long and highly positive profile of him in the business section of *The New York Times*. So I want to amend my advice from the previous book: It's often necessary to boast, but it's even better if others do it for you.

7. Success breeds success. The best way to impress people is through results. It's easier for me to do deals now because I've had so many triumphs. You have to create success to impress people in the world of business. If you're young and you haven't had any successes yet, then you have to create the impression of success. It doesn't mat-

ter whether the success is a small one or a big one—you have to start with something and build on it.

8. Friends are good, but family is better. It's better to trust your family than your friends. When I was young, I said to someone who had a fairly big business, "Do you see your brothers and sisters?" The person looked at me and said, "Yes, I do, Donald. I see them in court." That had a big impact on me, and I've always tried to stay close to my brothers and sisters, my children, and my former wives.

9. Treat each decision like a lover. Vast fortunes are accumulated through dozens of decisions a day, thousands a month, and hundreds of thousands in a career. Yet each decision is different and special in its own way. Sometimes you decide immediately—love at first sight. Sometimes you go slowly—the long engagement. Sometimes you gather people in a room and consider various opinions—the equivalent of asking your friends what they think of the person you've been dating. If you treat each decision like a lover—faithfully, respectfully, appropriately—you won't be locked into a rigid system. You'll adapt to the needs of that particular decision. Sometimes you'll think with your head. Other times you'll think with other parts of your body, and that's good. Some of the best business decisions are made out of passion.

Sometimes people are surprised by how quickly I make big decisions, but I've learned to trust my instincts and not to overthink things. I like to compare a decision to a lover because it reminds me to keep in touch with my basic impulses, the drives that excite us, attract us, give us inspiration and energy. We are all drawn to beauty, whether it's the allure of a person or the elegance of a home. Whenever I'm making a creative choice, I try to step back and remember my first shallow reaction. The day I realized it can be smart to be shallow was, for me, a deep experience.

10. Be curious. A successful person is always going to be curious. I don't know why this is true, but it's definitely the case. You have to be alive to your surroundings and hungry to understand your immediate world. Otherwise, you'll lack the perspective to see beyond yourself. One of the great aspects of working on *The Apprentice* has been learning about how network TV works. I recently found out that one of the reasons Thursday nights are so crucial to the networks is because that's when lucrative movie advertisements for the weekend releases are aired. The higher the ratings are on Thursday night, the more the networks can charge their advertisers. And the more they can charge their advertisers, the more they can pay me to save their network! You see? Curiosity pays!

I'll offer a lot more advice on how to think like a billionaire in the following pages. For the first time, I'm sharing practical advice on how to invest in real estate—buying, selling, getting a mortgage, dealing with a broker, renovating, and decorating. I've also put together a consumer guide to the best things in life. You don't have to be a billionaire to afford them, either.

Whenever I give speeches or appear in public, people want to hear about *The Apprentice*, so I'll take you behind the scenes of the first two seasons and describe what it's like to go from prime locations to prime time.

I'll never forget what a thrill the first season's live finale was. We were about to switch from the taped part of the show to the live conclusion, where, without a script, I would spontaneously announce whether I was hiring Kwame or Bill. Right before I went on the air, the brilliant head of NBC, Jeff Zucker, told me he was already receiving instant reports that the audience watching our program was going to be huge. That wasn't exactly what I needed to hear before appearing on live national television, but it turned out to be a truly exhilarating experience.

People have been referring to *The Apprentice* as a "comeback" for me, but I never went away. I was always big. And my buildings just keep getting bigger—and better!

And if you personally are bigger than ever, I've added another new element to this book: "The Mar-a-Lago Diet," a brief guide to the eating habits of billionaires and the people who lunch with them. I'm a frequent follower of the Mar-a-Lago Diet, and even though I'm not going to be considered thin, without this diet, I'd look and feel like a total disaster.

So turn the page and begin reading the only book I'll ever write that will make you rich *and* thin. Perhaps one day you'll join the billionaire's club. I'm sure I'll enjoy your company.

PART I

Real Estate

When people hear the name Trump, they think of two things: wealth and real estate. So while this entire book is dedicated to the creation and enjoyment of wealth, I need to start with the basics. The basics, for me, are all about property. Real estate is at the core of almost every business, and it's certainly at the core of most people's wealth. In order to build your wealth and improve your business smarts, you need to know about real estate.

What follows is some great advice. There are some helpful tips here for first-time apartment renters as well as for multiple-home owners. So read on.

How to Pick a Location

I hate the phrase "location, location, location" because I've seen a lot of idiots ruin good locations and a lot of geniuses make incredible investments out of horrible locations. You could hand over the location for Trump Tower (by far, the best location in New York City), and a moron could run the site into the ground. I guarantee it.

But when it comes to your home, you should always pick a good spot. Spending more on a good location is far smarter than getting a bargain in a bad area. Is it close to work? Is the neighborhood safe, or will you fear for your life as you come and go? Is it close to conveniences such as restaurants, grocery stores, shops, and banks? Do you feel like you belong in the neighborhood, or do you feel out of place? I'm the first to admit that location should be considered seriously when investing in real estate. A lot of picking a location comes down to instinct. You have to believe in the location; otherwise, you'll be making a rotten investment.

Be honest with yourself about the location's proximity to the rest of your life. If you find an apartment or a house or an office you like that puts hours of additional travel into your day, or requires expensive deliveries and services, or prevents people from visiting you, you might as well find somewhere else. I realize that not everyone can live and work in Trump Tower (which certainly works for me), but given the choice, you should find the location that works best for you.

Walk around in the neighborhood. Spend time there. What's the pattern of the day? When does the neighborhood wake up and when does it go to bed? What sort of people are living there and working there? Also, make sure to check it out on the weekends. Some neighborhoods in Manhattan are insanely busy all week and then dead all weekend, and vice versa. What happens if you move into an apartment and realize that there's a nightclub across the street blasting music each and every night or that garbage trucks congregate there after making the rounds in the early morning? You'll either go crazy or move out, neither of which are good options.

The view is important. I don't know anyone who wants to spend their life looking into an air shaft or a brick wall. If you have the option, go for the view. But you have to be careful with a view, particularly if you're paying for it. The current view might look out over a parking facility or an empty lot, but that could change in a week. In cities like New York, buildings seem to be going up at the rate of one per day, so make sure you have a good idea that the view there today will be there tomorrow.

When you're speculating or investing in real estate that will not necessarily serve as your primary home or office, I often advise finding space in a marginal neighborhood, buying or renting at a lower price, and then waiting for the neighborhood to improve. You'll save in taxes, make a meaningful contribution to the redevelopment of an area, and stand to make more money in the long run. If you have the time, the patience, and the fortitude, I recommend it. After all, when I bought up the West Side yards, people thought I was insane, but I've proved them wrong, as my development there can attest. Today that area is one of the most desirable and valuable areas in all of Manhattan.

How to Rent
an Apartment

A lot of people don't take renting an apartment as seriously as they should. I don't understand those people. While renting an apartment is not buying, the place will serve as your home and should be considered carefully. Not only is your home a big part of the way you feel about yourself, it's also a reflection of how others see you. Billionaires, even those who rent their homes, take time when finding places to live, and so should you.

In New York City, an apartment market I know all too well, people often feel lucky to find anything. There's enormous demand, and sometimes hundreds of people will charge through the streets to look at exorbitantly expensive shoe boxes that they all saw listed in *The New York Times.* Most of these people will be prepared—with letters of reference, with bank statements and credit card bills, and with a sense of competition that can be fierce. To play in this apartment market, or any other real estate market, you have to do your homework. Have a clear idea of your financial needs and your living requirements. Going blindly from apartment to apartment will be a waste of everyone's time—particularly your own.

I feel strongly that an apartment should be rented with the help of a good broker. It can be done without one, but to me, that's like taking pills without consulting a doctor or filing a lawsuit without a lawyer. It's possible, but it's stupid. Brokers know the neighborhoods and the specific markets inside and out. They know property values, the pros and cons of certain buildings, the rules and regulations of pricing and rents, and the ins and outs of the actual lease. Brokers are educated and licensed, and there's good reason for that. They will prevent you from making mistakes that will cost you thousands, and in my case, millions, more than the fees that they charge. They will also save you time by filtering out apartments that do not meet your criteria.

But you should never believe everything a broker tells you. The broker is, after all, only there for the commission, as concerned and accommodating as he or she may seem. And when it comes to the commission, whether you're selling, buying, or renting, always negotiate. Sometimes brokers do an amazing job and deserve a high commission, but when you enter the relationship, always negotiate from the start. It's much easier to negotiate the fee at the beginning of a broker relationship. Trying to lowball brokers midway through or at the end of a transaction is poor business form.

If you cannot afford a broker or simply want to go it alone, look in the papers or on bulletin boards. Ask around and walk around. Some of the best New York stories I've heard are about finding apartments that simply came out of nowhere—kind of like those stories about getting a taxi in the pouring rain on New Year's Eve. It can happen, but the odds are lousy. In *When Harry Met Sally,* Billy Crystal reads through the obituaries so he can move in on the apartments of the recently deceased. If you want to go without a broker, maybe try that approach, as morbid as it might sound.

Whether or not you use a broker, find somewhere you'll be happy for a long time. Moving around every couple of years is disruptive and expensive. And most important, figure out what you can afford. It's not a concern for me, but I would never spend more than twenty-five percent of my salary on rent—no matter how fantastic an apartment you have found. Every dollar you pour into rent is a dollar you could be using elsewhere—whether it's for savings, or for utilities, or for enjoying the finer things in life. It's okay to stretch yourself slightly and anticipate that in a few years you may be making more money, but that's not a sure thing—and it's a safe assumption that your rent will increase at the same rate as your salary. Tenants who cannot pay their rent will go nowhere fast—and certainly never make it into the billionaires club.

How to Read
a Classified Ad or Listing

Often people resort to the classified ads or other listings to find apartments and houses for rent. Don't be a fool! In New York, in particular, advertisers will make rat-infested closets sound like the penthouse of Trump Tower. Learn to see through the garbage in the advertisements so you don't waste time looking at apartments that should be bulldozed rather than inhabited. The advertisers should all write novels, since they're clearly so talented at writing fiction.

Pay attention to words like "funky" and "charming," which you can translate as "unlivable" and "run-down." Ads that brag "newly renovated" usually mean that the landlord has simply slapped new knobs on the bathroom cabinets. Other phrases that should make you nervous include "old-world appeal" (read: "dilapidated"), "cozy" (read: "tiny"), and "freshly painted" (read: "There's nothing good to say about the apartment except that it has a fresh coat of paint"). Anything that sounds too good to be true *is*—especially when it comes to apartments.

Also, pay attention to the information that's not provided. If there's no apartment number given, you can bet it's on the first floor (where it's never good to live because of crime and noise), and if there's no square footage provided, it's too embarrassing for the advertiser to mention. Also, if there's no photograph, beware. Even the worst apartments can be made to look palatial on film, so you should be doubly suspicious if a photograph is missing when other apartments in the ad include one.

Houses, apartments, and offices need to be touched and seen before you rent or buy them. Classified ads and listings can point you in the right direction, but it's your responsibility to thoroughly investigate any property you may be considering.

How to Buy a House

The real estate market can be terrifying, which is part of the reason I love it so much. But it can be downright petrifying when it involves what may be your most valuable possession: your home. The market changes every day, sometimes every minute. For home buyers, some of whom will buy one house in a lifetime, trying to time the market perfectly can be a ridiculous waste of time. In ten, twenty, or forty years, any small variations in the price of your house will have amortized into a blip on your financial radar screen.

You have to go with your gut, and if you love a house and you can afford it and your broker assures you that you are paying a fair market price, you're paying the best price. It's as simple as that. When it comes to your home, don't be concerned about spending more than it's worth if you know that you will be there forever and you'll be happy there. Sometimes the emotional price you put on a house may exceed the market price. Buying a home is different from the pure economics of investing in real estate. If you simply cannot afford a house that you love, don't be shy about underbidding; sometimes the seller will surprise you.

Before you start looking for a house, or even figuring out what you can afford to buy, make sure you have money socked away. Brokers and sellers will take you seriously, and you will increase your bargaining power as you're able to increase the size of your down payment. Buying a house is a serious investment, and banks and lenders will be there to help you make that investment.

A typical home buyer will not have access to one hundred percent financing, and you have to be as invested as your lender. The down payment should be your own personal gauge for your commitment to the house. Don't lose sight of the checks and balances because ultimately it will all come down to *your* checks and balances.

While it's good to be mindful of costs when buying a house, don't go overboard. Don't try to save money on necessary items, such as not getting a survey where it might be of value, or relying on people who are not well recommended or not known. Do not attempt to save small amounts of money on items that are important parts of the process. People often stupidly try to save money at a real estate closing, since some adjustments will probably still be made and the negotiations will not have ended. But don't be hardheaded and cheap when it comes to buying a house. It's counterproductive.

Simply put aside some money before you begin the house-buying process (call it your reserve budget), and then legal and financial situations that arise will not be skipped to cut costs. Undermining the purchase of your home from the beginning will only end up haunting you down the line.

How to Get an Appraisal
and a Building Inspection

Let's say you find your dream home. A perfect location, perfect architecture, perfect price. Be careful. Always know what you are mortgaging. Don't let your guts trick your brain, and don't rush yourself (or allow your broker—who will always be telling you about the other buyers—to rush you, either). It is better to have researched the opportunity and lose it than to make a mistake by jumping into something you'll come to regret.

The best reality check is the appraisal. The lender will have an appraiser, and in most situations, you will be responsible for paying for the appraisal. The appraisal should not be seen as an annoying expense that will only benefit the lender. The appraisal benefits you as well. Appraisers are professionals, and they will be able to see things that may elude the eye of most home buyers. Ask questions and do your own homework, but at the end of the day, defer to the appraiser. Some of his or her findings might be insulting or surprising, and the truth can hurt, but the appraiser's job is to be objective. A fair appraisal will only help you in the end.

Any number of things—some of which are regulated by the government (such as flood control)—can affect the location. Other factors, such as proximity to high-tension wires, may or may not be so apparent. You're probably not going to wind up buying the Amityville Horror, but you shouldn't expect that every seller will tell you everything unfavorable about the property. You're better off assuming that some things will not be divulged, out of ignorance, forgetfulness, or evasion. If you're confused by what I'm telling you, rent the movie *The Money Pit* to familiarize yourself with the pains of ignoring or forgoing the appraisal.

In the event that a structure is being purchased with mortgage funds, most probably you should also have a building inspector examine the premises. A building inspection is often required, but you should always require it for yourself. A knowledgeable, licensed inspector-engineer can detect whether the heating unit is functioning properly, whether the air-conditioning is sufficient, whether a sump pump is needed, and so on. Think of a building inspection as an X ray; the inspector will be able to see through the entire house and identify any systemic problems. For instance, what sort of materials were used for a house's piping? Galvanized? Brass? Copper? Synthetic? Galvanized pipes rust and don't last as long as brass pipes, which don't last as long as copper pipes, which don't last as long as synthetic pipes. Only a building inspector will be able to see this level of detail within a house or apartment.

If the inspector makes you nervous or you sense that he or she is working too quickly, find someone else. The inspection is too important to be careless about it.

Sometimes the problems inspectors find are fixable at a reasonable cost, but other times they find things that cannot be fixed without major renovations or even a teardown. The inspector will provide an objective, independent report that may or may not affect the value of the home, but either way, you can request price adjustments based on the inspection.

Another quick tip: Some investors make the dumb mistake of assuming that new constructions do not require building inspections.

Wrong! New constructions often have the largest problems, particularly if the build-out and contracting were sloppy. In addition to structural, plumbing, and electrical woes, new constructions can be vexed by mold infestation and other problems typically associated with longer-standing buildings.

How to Sell a House

If you are selling your home and there is no or little activity, or activity but no offers, you should revisit the price. The real estate market is volatile, and prices change daily. I always keep in mind the saying "Old listings, like old soldiers, never die—they just fade away" when it comes to pricing. Also, don't worry about competition; count on it—you will save yourself a lot of time. Competition may even help you by drawing in prospective buyers within the same market.

If you know your property is valuable, remain patient. As long as you're realistic about its value, there will always be a buyer eventually. Mar-a-Lago was sitting there a long time before I saw it and decided to move on that magnificent site. I had the right vision for it, and the timing was right for me—and, ultimately, for the seller as well.

Just make sure what you have to offer *is* the best, and you need not worry. If you have a broker, make sure he or she understands what the value of the property is to *you*. But don't be too bullheaded if your broker thinks the property is worth far less than you do. The broker should be the expert, and you're paying him or her not only for service but for advice.

Your broker, if he or she is good at the job, will strategically advertise the property's sale. A lot of interest is not necessarily always a good thing; be wary of a broker who fails to screen applicants and lets the whole world traipse through your house. Good brokers will screen applicants for prequalification, negotiate on your behalf for the best price, and facilitate the legal and financial processes. You will be paying the broker a substantial fee (usually on the order of six percent and sometimes higher), so he or she is working for you and should be working hard for that commission.

Some people try to sell houses without brokers—not a strategy I would recommend. But if you're feeling up to it, by all means, be my guest. If you want to be your own broker, then the best piece of advice I have is: Act like a broker. To do so will require a lot of guts, a lot of brains, and a lot of patience.

An article by Lynnley Browning entitled "The Sweet and Sour of 'For Sale by Owner,' " in the June 6, 2004, edition of *The New York Times,* made it clear just how difficult (but also how money-saving) selling your own home can be. You should find her article and maybe pick up some books to help you along the way. You will have to educate yourself on title searches, legal forms, and the pricing market; you will also have to learn your state's disclosure laws to avoid being sued if the ceiling caves in or mold takes over after you have left. It all sounds like a headache to me, which is why I've always recommended using a broker.

How to Find a Good Office

Location is probably the most important concern when it comes to finding a good office. Traveling for meetings, delivering goods and services, and attracting customers and clients can be a hassle if you have a poor location. You, your customers, and your employees have to be happy and productive in that space, and cutting costs and choosing poor office space is a fast way to kill your business.

Think about the space you will need, hopefully with enough room for some expansion without requiring you to move within the too near future. If you can find raw space on the fringe of your desired location, this strategy could prove lucrative to you in the future. It may require more up-front time and planning on your part, but it can have enormous financial and professional benefits. Being ahead of the pack is the best place to be.

It's also important that you find an office in a building that's well maintained and well run. Is the landlord notorious for not fixing the heat? Are the elevators operating efficiently and the bathrooms cleaned regularly? No one I know wants to spend time in an office—either working there or just doing business there—that's unattractive, uncomfortable, and inhospitable.

Where you work and what that space looks like are just as important as where you live, if not more. Give it the same thought, and you will be thankful you did. I've been in the same offices at Trump Tower for over twenty years. The location and the space work as beautifully today as they did twenty years ago. It's not dumb luck, though. I knew exactly where I would be today twenty years ago.

How to Deal with a Broker

Why have a novice try to understand the value of a great piece of art? Choose your broker as you would an art dealer—which is to say, judiciously. And as with many things, timing is crucial to success. Stay on top of things, and make sure you and your broker are honest with each other at each step in the process. A good broker will listen and respond to your concerns. If the broker takes days to return your phone calls or runs late to meetings, borrow my line and simply say, "You're fired!" There are countless other brokers who deserve your business. You're the customer, after all.

The best brokers know that whatever is good for you will be good for them. They make money only when you finally make a transaction, so the smart ones won't waste time trying to sell or rent something just for the sake of a commission. My advice is to find a reputable, established broker who has shown a substantial growth index over a number of years in the area in which you desire to live. As in all matters of life, brokers specialize. Why waste time with a broker who only knows high-end retail real estate when you're looking for an affordable one-bedroom apartment?

The best brokers are psychologists, or at least they are incredibly insightful. It's their job to figure out what's best for you, but in order for you to help them figure what is best for you, you have to be up-front and honest with them. Don't be embarrassed about telling them that you can't afford something or that you don't like a particular space. Experienced brokers tell me they can usually sense the people who are serious by their first two questions, and those are tip-offs on how to proceed.

Don't ever follow the advice of any broker who is pushy. That should be the indication for you to become wary. It isn't necessary for brokers to behave that way, and if they do, they are best left alone. I know some terrific brokers who are low-key, sincere, and genuinely interested in your well-being.

Susan James, who runs the sales office at Trump International Hotel and Tower, is one of the most elegant people you will ever meet, and her elegance isn't an act to get her into your good graces. She remains friends with her clients for many years after they are happily ensconced in their apartments. She is clear about what she is present-ing to you before, during, and after. That's the mark of a great broker.

Find a great broker and your chances of finding or selling the right place at the right price will be improved by about one hundred per-cent. The fee you pay will be one of the best investments you ever make.

How to Hire an Attorney

In some areas, attorneys are not ordinarily involved in real estate clos-
ings. In other areas, they absolutely need to be involved. If the cost is
reasonable, hire one, even if the situation seems simple. I never, ever
sign a contract without consulting an attorney, and I work with contracts all day long. Real property can involve complicated legal con-
cepts, some of which date back to feudalism. If you feel that the
situation is simple and you cannot afford to pay standard rates, most
attorneys will negotiate their fees. And if the situation turns complicated and a larger fee materializes, you shouldn't complain. You should
consider yourself lucky, since you have probably avoided some problems not otherwise foreseen.

How do you a get a good attorney, if you do not already know
one you can trust? Call any bar association, as they usually have referral services. Do *not* ask your mortgage broker to refer an attorney.
Though brokers always know many attorneys, there can be a built-in
conflict of interest if the sale deserves to be aborted. The lawyer
might be reluctant to recommend terminating the deal, since the

person who recommended him or her will then lose a commission. You're better off getting an independent recommendation for a lawyer who practices primarily in the area of the kind of real estate in discussion—someone who has a good reputation in the eyes of people you know and trust.

How to Get the Best Mortgage

Even billionaires need to borrow money now and then, and I've learned a lot about mortgages over the years. The first step is to know what you are mortgaging. I know that sounds obvious, but it's amazing to me how often people will seek a mortgage for something they clearly don't know the value of.

Numerous books have been written on how to get the best mortgage. Much of the advice is good, and much of it is common sense, and much of it is never properly acted upon. You can probably find a dozen books in your public library on mortgages, but what you really need to understand is how officers at banks and insurance companies think about loans, property, and you. Lenders can often make the most money off of idiots, so be sure to educate yourself before you see them.

Like buying a property, applying for a mortgage works best when you have options. Shop around, ask questions, and always bargain. There are countless choices in the mortgage market. The trick is finding the mortgage that works best for you—for your bank account, for your salary, and for your future plans. A mortgage is a product—like the house or the car that you're buying with it—so you should know its ins and outs before "purchasing" it. Drive a hard bargain and don't be afraid to walk away.

Loan officers can be schizophrenic, offering different rates and deals from one minute to the next. Never, ever accept a first offer, and always ask for better terms. Negotiate or be eaten alive! If you receive a better deal from Lender A, always go back to Lender B and see if they can match it. After all, each lender is peddling the same product—money—so it doesn't matter where it's coming from. Mortgages are designed to be haggled over, and not to do so is the equivalent of burning money in the street.

If you are buying or mortgaging a house or a multifamily dwelling, you have to know what the financials are. Certainly the mortgage company will have to know. Here are some recommendations:

1. Seek accounting advice. Your lawyer and mortgage broker can be of help, too.

2. Know the tax history of the property and also any foreseeable tax hikes. Good indicators of an impending tax increase include the need for a new school, a pending reassessment, a busted sewage system, or unpaid liabilities. Once you have taken on the burden of a mortgage, the last thing you'll need is a huge tax bill.

3. Look for hidden costs. There always are some, and they can sink you if you're not careful. Sound, comprehensive cost analysis is crucial. For instance, what if the building cannot be insured at ordinary rates? How do costs for heating, water, and extermination change throughout the year? Try to anticipate any scenarios that will put you in the thick of financial jeopardy.

At the end of the day, your mortgage company will want to know what you know. The mortgage company is there to help you. If the mortgage company isn't happy with a certain situation attached to the property, you should not be happy with it, either. Most likely, they have more experience than you and have seen other properties turn into nightmares once mortgaged.

Also remember that mortgage companies often sell their mortgages to other corporations, banks, insurance companies, or Fannie Mae; the people who are dealing with you initially may not be the same people you will be sending your monthly check to. For that matter, you may very well get notices to send your monthly check to different parties over a number of years.

Ordinarily, you will be personally responsible for any home mortgage, and there is a good chance that you will be required to place a personal guarantee on any investment mortgages. If you guarantee a mortgage, you could find yourself paying on a guarantee, even if you have prepared yourself thoroughly. Guarantees can be called upon due to the ups and downs of the market, weather-related catastrophes, and all sorts of insurance-related issues.

The subject of title insurance, which you should have to protect yourself against such frauds as forgery in a previous deed and other malfeasance, is also one you should discuss carefully with your attorney. Don't get caught unawares.

Real estate can afford great opportunities through mortgaging, leverage, and possibly even absentee management, but don't bet on it. Like anything else, it requires caution, devotion, hard work, and some luck. In truth, there is nothing complicated about mortgaging properties, but care and study are required.

Anyone who has seen those commercials on TV in the middle of the night where individuals claim to have retired to Hawaii on the basis of real estate purchased, sold, or rented should realize that the people who sell these courses make more money from selling the courses than they do from selling any real estate or mortgaging. Those infomercials never tell you about the mountain of problems that can be associated with the ownership of real estate.

How to Pick a Mortgage Broker

A good way to get a mortgage is to pass the buck to somebody else. Shopping around and comparing mortgages can be time-consuming, so it may save you time to pay someone to do your shopping for you. Get a mortgage broker, but get a good one. These people are engaged daily in the world of mortgages, which means that they have to know where to get the best rates, who is offering the best conditions, and generally, where it's advantageous to apply.

In the long run, you will probably pay less for everything if you get a good mortgage broker, since the broker will know what kind of hidden charges there are and steer you clear of various problems. Not only that, but mortgage companies want to keep in the good graces of anyone who is in the habit of referring business to them. There are certainly technical considerations, such as the length of the mortgage, whether guarantees are involved, conditions of default, and all kinds of other things that a mortgage broker and a good attorney will inform you about.

Ask your real estate broker to recommend a mortgage broker,

or get a referral from friends, colleagues, and neighbors who have recently taken on mortgages. Like your real estate broker or your attorney, the mortgage broker should be someone you feel comfortable working with—and someone you know will not sideline your best interests in favor of his or her own financial considerations.

How to Pick an Interest Rate and a Down Payment

Interest rates are not the mystery they're cracked up to be, but before you get into any real estate venture, you must educate yourself about them. I always think of interest rates simply as the "cost of money." The interest rate is like a yearly membership fee or a utility bill; it's the amount you're paying to use the mortgage per year. It's like a golf membership to an exclusive club where you're the only one with the keys to the clubhouse.

You should note that some institutions will try to trick you with adjustable interest rates so that your fees will bounce around, depending on the economy. If you're adverse to change and want to minimize your risk, I would recommend working with fixed rates. Interest rates have been sagging for the last twenty-odd years, and there's good reason to believe that they will only be going up in the short term. Mortgage holders with adjustable rates may be forced to foreclose if the payments become too big. If this setup scares you (and it should), lock in a rate that you know you'll be able to afford for the length of the mortgage.

When choosing an actual rate, if it's too good to be true, beware. Rates, truth be told, should actually not be the most important consideration, though certainly they need to be considered. To get the best rate today, there are all kinds of services and information available that can tell you what the various banks are charging. The Internet has exploded with information (but be careful, as not all of it is accurate). Newspapers often chart interest rates as well.

If you get a rate that is much lower than what is out there on the market, you might be looking for trouble. The company might not be around by the time you want to close the mortgage, or you might be charged outrageous fees for a closing. For any mortgage, the lender will also charge assorted fees, and it's wise to make sure you're not getting taken for a ride. A good rule to remember: The lower the interest rate, the higher the possible fees. Read the fine print. Look for a low rate, but remember that the lowest rate may end up costing you the most.

When it comes to a down payment, it should be determined in large part by your budget. A lower down payment will result in higher mortgage payments, and vice versa. Depending on where you live, the down payment will hover around twenty percent of the total loan. In New York City, where the competition for real estate is fierce, the percentages tend to be a lot higher. If you're a good negotiator and want to free up as much of your money as possible, you should try to get as low a down payment as possible.

How and When to Renovate

If you're going to mortgage a property that you already own, make sure it is in good condition. For a multifamily building, attention should be given to all kinds of things, such as the condition of the roof, stairways, elevators, storage areas, boiler room, and everything else. Suffice it to say, if the building is not in good condition, an experienced mortgage officer is not going to want to lend money on it. Nor will a bank lend you money on a structure if they do not believe you are going to preserve and protect their collateral. Why should they?

If you're about to mortgage your property, you should never make repairs just for cosmetic purposes. Make good, solid repairs and then sell the property or mortgage it for a lot more money. Fix the kitchen; redo the bathroom; put on a fresh coat of paint. My father used to say that every property ought to be sold in "mint condition." He said it to me all the time. We all know what it means, and it's some of the best advice he ever gave me. After all, a $15 can of paint can add $1,000 to the value of your property; $1,000 in landscaping can add $10,000; and $10,000 in remodeling can add $100,000. You get the idea.

In addition to renovating before selling a property, you may choose to renovate after buying or over the years while you're living or working somewhere to make the space more livable or workable. Renovation equals devotion. It can be expensive and time-consuming, so it's crucial that you figure out whether or not renovations will be worthwhile before committing to them. Renovation is worth it only if your heart and your checkbook are in it. If they're not, it will turn out to be one enormous hassle after another. After all, renovating can often be more difficult than building from scratch.

I have always found that the trickiest part of renovations is matching the original ingredients, which isn't always easy. Sometimes just finding them can require a lot of investigative work. I have an employee at Mar-a-Lago who spends his whole week, every week, just keeping up with the tile work on the premises. There are something like thirty-six thousand Spanish tiles at Mar-a-Lago, most of which date back to the fifteenth century. I know it might sound ridiculous, but the tiles alone require this kind of attention, and so they get it. You can't just let an investment like that deteriorate. Be prepared for this kind of devotion when you begin serious renovations.

The Mar-a-Lago Club is a classic example of smart renovation. In addition to historic merit and exquisite beauty, Mar-a-Lago has been a phenomenal investment—made even more priceless by the hard work that my staff and I have devoted to it. It's more than real estate or an investment; it's a piece of art that requires endless, painstaking work—work that's not only financially rewarding but somehow spiritually uplifting as well. I make sure everything done there is top-notch, because Mar-a-Lago is up there with Venetian palaces in terms of craftsmanship and beauty. It deserves the best.

The ceiling, the flooring, the walls, the chandeliers, the mirrors—you have to be insane about the details or the whole enterprise will fail. For instance, I've spent a good eight months choosing the right chairs for the ballroom being built at Mar-a-Lago. The ballroom is seventeen thousand square feet in area, so the chairs will be a big part of the room. I have seen probably hundreds of them by now. They have to be

just right or the effect will be lessened, if not spoiled. The gilt on them has to be compatible with the entire room, and their shape and comfort must be considered as well. You should be as attentive to details as I am, no matter what the scale of your project.

This point should be obvious, but I'll state it anyway: Never, never do serious renovations on a property that you're renting, or begin negotiating for renovations on a property before your mortgage closes. To do so is financially destructive and an absolute waste of time.

How to Landscape

Once you have found your home or your office, hire a reputable landscape firm to help you. It will add incredible value to the property. Trump Tower is one of the most visited buildings in New York City, and part of the attraction is the trees that decorate the building. If you've never been to New York, Trump Tower should be your first stop. It's breathtaking.

It's amazing. Trees, bushes, rocks, and flowers can turn the most mundane buildings into works of art. Landscaping can add value to a building far above the cost of labor and materials. If you can't afford a landscaper, do it yourself. I always joke that landscaping on your own is a win-win; it's cheap *and* good for your health.

If you hate physical labor, like I do, you'll hire someone. The trick is finding someone with your taste who can work within your budget and within your schedule. Remember that the cheapest is not always the best. As with contractors, shoddy work will need to be redone or, even worse, corrected, and that can be a disaster. When choosing a landscaper, find a firm with a good reputation by asking your neighbors or other business owners for recommendations.

Also, try to visit some sites where the landscaper has previously done work. If the work is shoddy, you'll know right away to find someone else. You can also check on the equipment that the landscaper is using. If the equipment is busted, the service will most likely be busted, too.

And finally, make sure the work that they're doing will last for years with minimal maintenance. No one wants to have to replant every year. A landscaper can do incredible work, but if it looks worn and dead within six months, you will have thrown your money away.

Of course, it helps to have a lot of money and clout. When I'm building and landscaping golf courses, I love to buy beautiful trees. Sometimes, though, those trees aren't in nurseries; sometimes they are in a person's backyard. I'll be driving down the highway, see a great tree, and ask my limo driver to pull over. I'll knock on the door. Usually, a woman will answer the door, and I'll say, "Hi, lady. I'd love to buy your tree." She'll say, "Oh my god! It's Donald Trump! I can't believe this is happening!" And then I'll tell her that I'm building a golf course nearby, like the one I'm building in Los Angeles right along the Pacific Ocean. Usually, I'll get the tree. I've bought a lot of great trees that way, and those trees can be found all over the country at my golf courses. Money can't buy happiness, but it sure as hell can buy some great trees.

How to Decorate Interiors

I feel the same way about interior decorators that I feel about real estate brokers. They are worth every penny. If you know your tastes, hire a professional who can help you fine-tune those tastes and work with you to create the perfect environment for your work or for your home.

If you see a space you like—whether it's a living space or a restaurant or an office—ask questions. Who was the architect? Who decorated it? Like hiring a broker or a contractor, hiring the right decorator works by word of mouth and by finding someone with your sensibilities. Make sure the designer has your best interests in mind, not merely their own. It's their job to know your tastes, whether innately or otherwise, and to find the best way to display them.

Most people incorrectly think that interior decorators are a wasteful extravagance, but believe me, they will save you time and money. Interior decorating is not as simple as walking into a furniture store and pointing at a couple of pieces. Good interior decorators have a talent for spatial configuration, choosing colors and materials, and, most important, negotiating. The best interior decorators have that rare mix of artistic talent and business smarts.

Even something as simple as choosing a carpet can require days and days of flipping through sample books. I can't think of anything more boring. Instead, good interior decorators will scour warehouses, antique shops, and furniture showrooms for you, and then come to you with a plan, including fabric, carpet, and paint samples, as well as layouts and themes. With the best interior decorators, you just sit there and say, "Ah, that's perfect. I never would have thought of that."

Most decorators work on commission (anywhere from ten to fifteen percent, and sometimes as high as twenty or twenty-five percent). Instead of grumbling about the commission, look on the bright side. Not only do decorators save you time (and in the end, money, since you won't make as many mistakes), but dealers and warehouses always extend decorators discounts not available to the average consumer. They can pass those savings on to you. Simple math tells you that it's better to pay a commission on a sofa that's marked down to a professional discount of fifty percent than on the full price. For instance, if a decorator finds a $2,000 sofa that she can buy at a discount for $1,000, at a commission of twenty percent, you'll be paying $1,200 for that sofa. Even an idiot can see what's a better deal. And of course, more expensive tastes result in even bigger savings. Still, negotiate the commission down.

When you are working with a decorator, make sure you ask to see all of the invoices. Decorators are by nature honest people, but you should be double-checking regardless. It's okay to question them on certain expenditures, but don't haggle too much, because high-quality materials cost money. High-quality interiors last for years and years, so cutting corners will only lead to disrepair and an unattractive interior that you will have to live with—or change, at even more expense.

Once I hired a decorator whose portfolio of work had impressed me. I was busy at the time and didn't spend a great deal of time with the designer or watching the progress of his work. I just assumed the work would be on par with the portfolio. The results were a nightmare. I tried to live with the work, but after one month I couldn't stand it anymore and everything was taken out. I had to start all over. It cost me a small fortune, but it did teach me a lesson I learned once and have never had to repeat: First, find the right person, and second, monitor his or her progress.

How to Deal with Contractors

If you think real estate brokers and interior decorators make you nervous, you should spend a day with me when I'm working with contractors. They are like racehorses—they can be as lazy as all get out, and then they can race to the finish line and surprise you. There's not much in between. They can really be difficult to handle, but if you prepare yourself, you'll have a much better experience working with them. Always remember that they will try to get away with as much as they possibly can. If you call them on it, they'll shape up. They're a strange bunch—and I won't be offending anyone by saying that, because they know it as well as I do.

Some of them can work wonders and will do so eventually. Some of them won't work wonders ever, which you will also find out eventually. That's why it's good to pick contractors you already know or who have a good record on their past jobs. If you're new to the business of hiring contractors, ask neighbors, friends, and colleagues about contractors they've worked with. Nine out of ten will tell you horror stories, and if they don't, get the contractor's name and put it to use.

Always get references from contractors. Ask the contractor to give you ten names of other jobs they have done within the last year. Jobs that they did four or five years ago are not good measures; the jobs need to be recent. And don't ask for just two names; ask for the full ten. It's easy to make two parties happy, but only a great contractor can make ten parties happy.

Once you've hired a contractor and negotiated a budget, my best advice for you is to be tough on them. If you're not, they'll think you're soft and a pushover. You have to make your expectations clear. Be clear and up front about timing and the inflexibility of your budget. If you need the job finished by a certain time, hold the contractors to that date. If you keep an eye on their work and act as knowledgeable as possible, you increase the chances that the contractors will respect you and get something done.

I knew some contractors who took two months to finish renovating a single shower because they had so many "emergencies" at home that they couldn't seem to get anything done. The poor couple believed every sob story and would even give the contractors home-made cookies, brownies, and lasagna for their unfortunate friends and families. These contractors gained about ten pounds each, and not until the couple figured out what was going on did they manage to finish the shower—in less than two days. It's amazing—and sometimes criminal—what goes on in the world of contractors.

How to Make Sure Your Property Appreciates in Value

Appreciate your property, and your property will appreciate for you. If I visit one of my buildings, and I see something out of place—something that only the most discerning of eyes would be able to spot—I make sure it's fixed immediately. Chipped paint, an upholstery stain, a missing lightbulb—if you do not stay on top of the maintenance, the property will deteriorate quickly. Small problems multiply.

You owe it to yourself and to your community to make your property the best it can be. All that work and devotion are combined into a single manifestation of creativity, energy, economics, and talent. A great building is an emblem of the time and people that produced it. It represents the economics and the spirit of the era in which it was built. Buildings can be enormous contributions to society that will remain long after our time here and, if built right, will garner more and more value as time goes by.

So not only is it a crucial step to becoming a billionaire, but guaranteeing that your property appreciates in value is also a civic responsibility. I am a committed philanthropist to many charities, but perhaps my greatest gifts have been the buildings and properties that I have bestowed on various communities. Increasing the value of a single property has a ripple effect in the community around it. All of the buildings that bear the Trump name have made their environs more valuable—not just economically but culturally as well.

Beyond the steps you can take to increase the value of your property (landscaping, interior decoration, renovation), you also need to work with your neighbors to make sure they have the same goals as you. My advice: Join or form a neighborhood association. Neighborhood associations help control crime and traffic, maintain parks and other recreation spaces, and monitor the efficiency of services such as litter pickup and recycling.

You're only as good as your surroundings. You can have the best Brioni suit in the entire world, but if it's paired with some crappy shoes and an awful tie, the Brioni suit is pretty much worthless. It's the same for properties. I often see a nice house alongside another house that's badly maintained—it hasn't been painted, the grass is uncut, a broken-down car is rusting in front of it. That's a huge negative for a homeowner, so you have to work with your neighbors to keep up your investment.

Also, if you see the value of your property being threatened, write letters to your politicians. Just the other day I wrote a letter to Mayor Bloomberg about the deplorable conditions on Fifth Avenue in Manhattan. The street vendors are ruining the street's image. They claim to be veterans so they can receive exemptions to peddle trinkets and souvenirs, but only a few of them actually are veterans. Do you see street vendors on the Avenue Montaigne in Paris? I don't think so.

PART II

Money

When you have a lot of money, it can cause misery. But I'd rather have that kind of misery than the misery without it.

Money may not grow from trees, but it does grow from talent, hard work, and brains. I have a talent for making money; some people don't. But part of my "talent" is my drive and my work ethic, so even if you don't have the genetic makeup to be a billionaire, you can still work hard and maybe, if you're lucky and smart, you can be a millionaire. Maybe you can even be a billionaire.

I won't deny that some people are luckier than others. That's a simple fact of life. But you can create luck. I remember one night, when I was billions of dollars in debt and the media that had at one point called me brilliant was now making me out to be a total dope, I had to be at a dinner party that I wanted to skip in the worst way. I just didn't feel up to it, but something inside me made me get up and go.

At the dinner that night, I ended up sitting next to one of many bankers. It was one of the luckiest nights of my life. He gave me some great advice and pointed me in a new direction. The rest is history. So when it comes to money, even if you're broke or in debt, your luck can change. You have to work hard to make that luck change, so keep reading to learn how to do just that.

How to Be a Good Investor

Good investing requires financial intelligence. Billionaires are often blessed with a high financial IQ. Most of them could be considered financial geniuses. But your financial IQ is not a fixed number, and you can improve it each and every day. My financial IQ is constantly improving as I watch over my many businesses and my staff. I work hard to make sure that they remain assets, not liabilities, and you should look at your holdings in the same way.

Having a degree from Wharton and a lifetime of investing experience, I will explain a few things for those who haven't been blessed with such advantages. Finance and business are a complex mix of components that embrace a large spectrum of enterprises. I think of it the way an artist thinks about technique. You need to have a basic technique before you can apply it to different media such as drawing, or sculpture, or painting. As a builder, I use my financial technique as a basic blueprint for increasingly complex transactions. Over the years, those blueprints have become larger and more complicated—and also more profitable.

Good investors are good students. It's as simple as that. I spend hours each day reading the financial media (*The Wall Street Journal, Forbes, BusinessWeek, Fortune, The New York Times, Financial Times*). I also read a lot of books and other magazines; you never know where your next great idea is going to come from. You should be on top of all the news within your industry and, beyond that, all local, national, and global news as well. Ignorance in current affairs can go a long way toward destroying your credibility—and your bank account.

People always ask what I like to watch on television. Typically, I only watch television that I know will improve my financial IQ. My one indulgence when it comes to television is sports. For news and financial advice, of course, I watch *The Apprentice,* but I also watch the CNBC business report, Larry King, Bill O'Reilly, the *Today* show, and Fox Cable. Whatever you watch or read, study something every day. It's essential that you keep your mind open and alert.

And if you're young, don't think you don't have the experience to come up with good investment ideas. I had some of my best ideas when I was twenty-two years old. When you're that young, you don't censor yourself as much, and ideas that you may have will not be clouded by your business experiences. Genius is the ability to assemble in new forms what already exists, and sometimes the youngest people are the greatest geniuses.

If you're still in school, pay attention. Education is a money machine. If you're long gone from school, consider enrolling in a financial education class. Some financial courses can be dry, but I always made them more interesting by applying the principles immediately to some project, either imaginary or real, that I could work through in my mind. That way, I was already getting real life experience while I was still in school.

How to Follow
Market Indicators

A savvy investor is a sponge for information. You have to read the news-papers, watch the news, and listen to the world carefully as it spins around you. You have to follow the market each and every day—and not just your own holdings, but globally. It's a huge task, and it takes years of practice to be able to synthesize information in the way the best investors do. Though recent events in finance have given us businesspeople a bad name, most of us are highly educated and hardworking. Most of us are not money-grubbers, as the media would have you believe.

Good investors use market indicators for two reasons: (1) to evaluate how they have done in the past, and (2) to make better predictions about how the market will perform in the future. If the Dow Jones or Nasdaq or the S&P always seems to be trouncing your own portfolio, then con-sider making changes in your investments or turning your money over to a money manager. If, instead, you're always ahead of most market indi-cators, you can start to watch for trends. If the Nasdaq rallies, how does that affect the bond market? If housing starts are down one month, what effect does that have on lumber prices or mortgage rates? The market is a crazy, interconnected monster, and you have to know how a change in one part will affect the whole beast—otherwise, it will clobber you.

How to Divide Up
Your Portfolio

If you are in a position to have a portfolio (even if it's just $10,000), it's a good idea to consult with experts. It's a tricky business, and the experts, though not magicians, can do a much better job than you at managing money. They spend all day tracking the markets, so trust them. A lot of idiots went crazy over dot-coms and start-ups, thinking they could make millions, and most of them lost everything.

I consider myself a savvy investor with billions to prove it, but even I wouldn't dare to strategize about my portfolio by myself. The fees that the experts charge will be zilch compared to the money you can make, especially if you find a trusted investor on your behalf. It's worth it. Your money can work for you if you put it in the right hands.

Sometimes the more money you pay a money manager, the more money he or she will make for you; don't be wooed by cheap advice, because your money may not go anywhere. Some advisers charge a fee as a percentage of profits; others charge by the hour or per meeting. Make sure that whomever you decide to use is honest and up front about the services that he or she will be providing you.

To find a trusted, competent financial adviser, I would consult people who live and work in the same area you do—and that may be in the same income bracket. Working with someone whose primary client base is in a vastly different bracket is not the best course to take. The National Association of Personal Financial Advisors is a good source of listings. They can be reached by phone at 800-366-2732 or online at www.napfa.org. If you feel nervous about an adviser, you can check to see whether others have complained, or make a complaint yourself, with the Certified Financial Planner Board of Standards (CFPBS). You can contact the CFPBS through its website at www.cfp.net or by calling 888-237-6275.

If you're stubborn and refuse to hire someone to work with your money, go for it—but work to minimize your risk with a bunch of different investments. If you put all of your money into one stock or one building or one venture and then it crashes, you're broke. Plain and simple. I'm probably guilty of not having a diverse enough portfolio—after all, it's almost all real estate. But I have teams of people working for me, and I know from years of experience how to protect myself when the markets get rough.

Determining the right mix of cash, bonds, and stocks for your portfolio does not have to be tricky if you follow the formula that Eric Sacher, a financial guru within my organization, recommends. Start with one hundred percent of your assets; most likely you will be devoting this pot to a mixture of cash, bonds, and stocks. Take the one hundred percent as the number 100 and then subtract your age. Eric recommends that you devote your age as a percentage to cash and bonds and the remaining amount to stocks. That way, as you age, you minimize your exposure to stocks, which can be a lot riskier and a lot more volatile than bonds.

For example, let's say you're thirty years old, and you have $100,000 to invest. By Eric's formula, you would subtract 30 from

100 to arrive at the following allocation: $70,000 (or seventy percent) to stocks and $30,000 (or thirty percent) to bonds and cash. Each year, as you grow older, make changes to minimize your vulnerability to stocks by moving money into cash and bonds.

Obviously, you will need to consider other factors as well, such as market conditions and interest rates. In a hot stock market, you could consider elevating your stock allocation, and in a high-interest environment, I would recommend raising your bond and cash allocation. With this basic guideline to follow, an individual looking to invest some cash should be able to do so in a reasonable, and hopefully lucrative, manner.

You also have to invest with your own personal financial needs in mind. If you'll need your savings for a down payment or to pay for college in the short term, do not pay a lot of broker fees to lock away your money. Instead buy certificates of deposit (CDs) or another investment vehicle that will keep your money liquid and safe.

The worst thing you can do is be timid and let your money just sit in your savings account. It's pure waste. Your money should be at work at all times. You should think of your money as your staff; you wouldn't let your staff sit around, so don't let your money sit around, either. Even in the worst economy, there is no excuse for putting money under the bed.

How to Buy Stocks and Bonds

I am a firm believer that unless you have the inside scoop or a great investment adviser, the average investor is usually at a disadvantage. Therefore, three points of advice:

1. Do your homework before you invest. A dumb investor is a dead investor.
2. Hire an adviser if you can afford one, and always research what you are buying. Don't go for the hot tip or quick hit. Those types of investments usually end up in the trash can.
3. Buy companies only when you understand what they do. It is always easy to go with the herd and buy what everyone else is buying, but remember what happened to most of the dot-coms you bought? Stick to what you know.

Stocks and bonds are a dangerous game, so if you're in the market for them, my advice is to be judicious. They are the gambler's gamble. You'll win sometimes, and you'll lose sometimes. Remember that the house has the advantage, and I would be more comfortable gambling in one of my casinos than I would on Wall Street. After all, if a company falls apart, the stockholders and the bondholders are typically last in line at the junkyard. In my casinos, you'll be a lot more comfortable—and you'll probably win a bit more as well.

If stocks are irresistible to you, then always invest in ones that you understand. I understand real estate—the nitty-gritty terms of the deals but also the nearly indescribable forces that make the real estate market tick. I don't understand biotechnology or computers or lumber, so I'm not going to throw my money at those industries. If you're already gambling, why play a game where you don't even understand the rules? If, on the other hand, there are companies and industries you know, take your roll and go.

When picking stocks and bonds, the bottom line should be the people involved. There are some great companies with some great products, but if a klutz comes on to run the show, the company is doomed. If a pharmaceutical company develops a pill that extends life by a hundred years and everyone goes nuts, the company will still fail if a loser is in charge. So pick your stocks like you would pick your surgeon. You're not going to have an incompetent operating on you, so don't have an incompetent tending to your money.

And then look closely at the numbers. The company should be growing by leaps and bounds each year. If a company's profits have been growing by only a small amount per year—or even losing money—ditch the stock or bond and invest in something else. Since the risks of the stock and bond markets are so enormous, you should be playing only if the rewards outweigh the risk. And always remember that the proof is in the pudding. CEOs will make promise after promise about future performance, but if the results haven't been delivered before, don't expect them to be delivered next time. Sell the stock or bond and move on.

How to Spot a Fraud

There's a simple rule here: If it seems too good to be true, it is. That rule should weed out a lot of "opportunities" immediately. The world is filled with scoundrels looking to make a dishonest buck, and when it comes to your money, you have to protect it from them. When making investments, particularly with unknown parties or in untested industries, make sure you do your homework. If you're prudent and cautious, you won't be swindled.

Often, charlatans will try to rip investors off by advertising a "new venture" that's dressed up in smart-sounding rhetoric and promises that are too good to be true. Just because you don't understand something doesn't make it a good investment.

Some people come up with the craziest investment opportunities. The other day I heard a rumor that pharmaceutical companies may try to develop a pill that would make cheating men and women monogamous. Sort of the opposite of Viagra. Some scientists studied voles, and they gave promiscuous male voles a special hormone shot that stopped them from straying. If humans took this kind of hormone, a cheating spouse could say to his or her spouse, "Oops. I forgot to take my medicine today."

But all joking aside, don't trust anyone who needs your money for a new venture. The words "new venture" sound to me like a loan that will never get paid back. That's my advice, even if the new venture is for a monogamy pill. They want your money, pure and simple, so they'll have a chance to make money. If you aren't entrepreneurial enough to create the venture, I'd recommend finding a safer way to invest.

How to Pinch Pennies

When *Spy* magazine started years ago, they decided to do a "Who Is the Cheapest Millionaire?" test. They sent checks in amounts from fifty cents to five dollars to a list of millionaires throughout the country. I received a check for fifty cents, and we at the Trump Organization deposited it. They may call that cheap; I call it watching the bottom line. The higher you climb on the list of billionaires, the cheaper people become. Every dollar counts in business, and for that matter, every dime. Penny-pinching? You bet. I'm all for it.

Penny-pinching is the opposite of being wasteful. I have never liked waste, whether it's time, effort, or money. I think I inherited this attitude from my parents, who were careful with everything, particularly money. I still don't like to overspend for anything, and I will always take the time to compare prices, whether I'm buying a car or toothpaste.

As I said before, I always sign my checks, so I know where my money's going. In the same spirit, I also always try to read my bills to make sure I'm not being overcharged. There is human (and now computer) error everywhere—at restaurants, at the phone company, at the grocery store, at hotels—and you'd be surprised by how much this human error can cost you. Don't be obsessive about it, but check through your bills from time to time.

You should also always feel comfortable bargaining for goods and services. I do it all the time, and I'm one of the richest men on earth. Even in high-end shops, I bargain. After all, the more you're paying for something, the more the seller should be able to shave off the price. I hate paying retail, and it makes me cringe when I see other people doing it. I've walked into stores and offered $2,000 for a $10,000 item. It can be embarrassing for me (especially since everyone knows that I'm Trump and that I'm wealthy), but you'd be amazed at the discounts you can get if you simply ask. You do have to be willing to walk away, but after you've walked away a few times, the price will come down. It's moronic to be too proud to save money.

Another way to pinch pennies is to avoid the brand names when it's necessary. I obviously buy brand names when the brand is tied to a product's quality. Golf equipment, jewelry, and clothing are good examples of brand as a signifier of quality. But aspirin is aspirin, shampoo is shampoo, and cereal is cereal, so don't throw away your money on packaging and advertising.

I understand that penny-pinching can have a negative connotation—as in "miserly"—but when you calculate how much ten cents on a price can matter if you multiply it by a hundred thousand or a million, the value of ten cents becomes clear. For instance, let's say I have to buy one hundred thousand lightbulbs for all of the buildings that I own and maintain each year. If I manage to save ten cents on each lightbulb, that's a savings of $10,000 per year! That's $10,000 I can put toward another building or another investment or donate to a cause that needs the money more than I do.

Pay attention to the small numbers in your finances, such as percentages and cents. Numbers that seem trivial add up and have enormous implications. My parents hammered frugality into me at an early age, and it's the most important money-management skill a person can use. Call it penny-pinching if you want to; I call it financial smarts.

How to Decide
How Much Risk to Assume
When Investing

It all comes down to one simple question: How much money can you stand to lose? That's how much risk you should assume. If you can't afford to lose it, play it safe. It's common sense, and it doesn't require a degree in finance to figure out.

You should never fall in love with your investments. If you do, you're in big trouble. Even if I think one of my buildings or resorts is absolutely the most spectacular place in the world (and most of the time they are), I still know when it's smart for me to move on to something else or keep it within my portfolio. It all comes down to your guts and your brains.

You need to watch the bottom line. Allen Weisselberg, my chief financial officer, has to be one of the toughest people in business when it comes to money. When I was having some financial problems in the early 1990s, I called Allen into my office and told him there would be tough times ahead. The banks were about to cut off our funding. Allen said, "No problem," and went back to his office, where he proceeded to renegotiate almost every payment from that point forward. He did whatever was necessary to protect the bottom line—and refused to succumb to the pressures of risk.

Now he's negotiating with bankers on deals worth hundreds of millions of dollars, and he's so tough that most banks would rather I negotiate the deal than him. He's a loyal employee, and he's the ultimate master at playing the cards of business.

To be a visionary and to be a billionaire, you have to chase impossibilities. Few ever get rich easily. So if you find yourself in a situation that you think is nearly impossible, ask yourself once more whether bailing is really the right decision. You never want to walk away and then see someone less deserving walk off with the pot.

For instance, I recently announced that my building at 40 Wall Street is up for sale for $400 million. That's an enormous price, and it's been a brilliant deal. I bought it in 1995 for only $1 million. It's a seventy-two-story 1929 landmark building, and now, sadly, the tallest building in the financial district. When I bought the building, it was completely empty, and I took on some enormous risk. People had given up on the financial district, and many said that my investment would be a failure. I stood by it. Today it's completely full, and I'll be selling it for at least four hundred times what I paid for it. Deal making doesn't get any better than that.

How to Stay on Top
of Your Finances

Periodically, I ask my financial department for what I call my financial "small shot." This report reflects, among other financial data, my cash balances, investments, sales of condominium units, and so forth. If I didn't check up on it regularly, I would be in big financial trouble, and I would have no one to blame but myself. You should pull yours together once in a while, too.

Keep track of your various positions, and when you see a trend you don't like, change it! Don't assume that your stocks are performing well or that your house is appreciating in value or that your business is growing just because someone tells you it is. Always look at the numbers yourself. If things turn grim, you're the one left holding the checkbook.

One day back in the late 1980s, Jeff McConney, my controller, prepared my small shot and brought it to me. I looked down at it and immediately told Jeff, "You're fired." I told him I didn't want excuses and I thought he was doing a lousy job managing my cash. Although I am a multibillionaire and I head a multibillion-dollar organization, every dollar spent by this company comes out of my pocket. The point I was making to Jeff was that even though various payments always need to be made, always question invoices and never accept a contractor's first bid. Negotiate! Negotiate! Or get out. Jeff got the message and has been with me for seventeen years and is doing a terrific job. He looks out for my bottom line as if the money were his own.

Whether you have someone managing your bottom line or you're doing it yourself, money, like anything, takes maintenance and planning to grow. Don't ignore it, because if you do, you're going to lose it.

How to Motivate Yourself Financially

I've met some brilliant businesspeople in my time, but some of them will never be billionaires because they never act on those brilliant ideas. Twenty percent of your priorities will give you eighty percent of your productivity. You should always focus your time, energy, and efforts on the top twenty percent of your priorities; that's a four-to-one return on your investment. So if you have a great idea, no matter how much work you know it will require, get going. Don't just sit there. There's nothing more criminal and self-destructive than having a great idea and then putting it off. As the saying goes, a slow starter is always the fastest finisher.

I once knew a guy who had terrific ideas, would talk them up at hurricane force, and then go off and putter away at something else. He would lose his momentum before he even got going. What's the point? He was the personification of the term "windbag," and I see and hear a lot of them every day. Maybe they're just entertaining themselves, and in that case they should be charging admission, because it's the only way they'll ever make a cent. Get a move on. Being rich isn't a passive state. Ultimately, time is more valuable than money, because if you run out of money, you can start over again. But when you've run out of time, there's no starting over.

How to Manage Debt

Debt needs to be managed, and the only person who can manage your debt is you. I always tell myself that I can put the leverage on or I can take the leverage off. I'm entitled to do either. Don't let your debt scare you into not doing anything. It should only invigorate you to work harder.

When I went through tough times financially, I used debt as leverage. I loved leverage, and leverage makes a lot of businesses both profitable and possible. But love of leverage when the market crashes is what ultimately eats you alive. I know the perils of too much debt better than anyone else, so believe me when I tell you that excessive debt is best avoided. I'm a much more conservative person now in terms of debt, and I would advise you to be conservative as well.

Debt can be managed if you thoroughly plan for contingencies and mishaps. Know the terms, the penalties, and the defaults associated with your debt. And if you do have debt, make sure you're using it proactively. Don't take on debt for regular expenses; debt should be used only to finance ventures and projects that will have a return to you. People with excessive credit card debt, for which the terms may be ridiculously inflated, are committing financial suicide.

If you do find yourself in debt, assess the full extent of the situation. How much debt are you in? How much are you paying each month to maintain that debt? What steps will you take to rid yourself of that debt?

Cut your expenses, shop for a refinancing tool that will allow you to maintain your debt at a lower interest rate, and make your minimum payments to avoid bad credit. If those steps don't work, then consult an expert in debt reduction. There may be alternatives that are not obvious to you.

How to Save and Pay
for College

The best time to start saving for your children's education is the day they are born, if not before. Good education isn't cheap, and it's crucial to guarantee that your children will have a fair shot in the world. Start a college savings account immediately.

If you are paying for your own education, look into grants and scholarships. There are a lot of them, and as a result of the high costs of education today, you may still be required to be creative in finding a way to make money while going to school. Don't gripe about having to work during school. It will be better for you in the long run, not only for your finances but for your character. You will graduate with a top-drawer education and work experience to boot.

It's also wise to consider from an early age what professions pay well, and plan accordingly. Physical professions—sports and so forth—are always risky and usually short-term in comparison to the length of a doctor's career or a lawyer's. You should also encourage your children (or yourself) to be honest about what makes them (or you) tick.

People often ignore their talents and opt for careers that don't suit them. That way only leads to failure. People should always be encouraged to follow their dreams (my children have) but realize that a lot of time and money can be wasted chasing dreams that just weren't meant to come true.

Life at the top is exactly as it seems—wonderful!
This is my apartment in Trump Tower.

*Melania on the night
of our engagement, at the
Metropolitan Museum of Art, NYC.*

Melania and me, out on the town.

Melania in our living room at Trump Tower.
Now, that's what I call statuesque beauty.

With Melania at a party for Gotham Magazine.

It doesn't matter where I am—the beat goes on.

Relaxing at my Mar-a-Lago Club in Palm Beach, Florida.

Melania and me with the one and only Tony Bennett.

Let's get down to business: familiar shots from The Apprentice.

V is for victory—and for the view from my office.

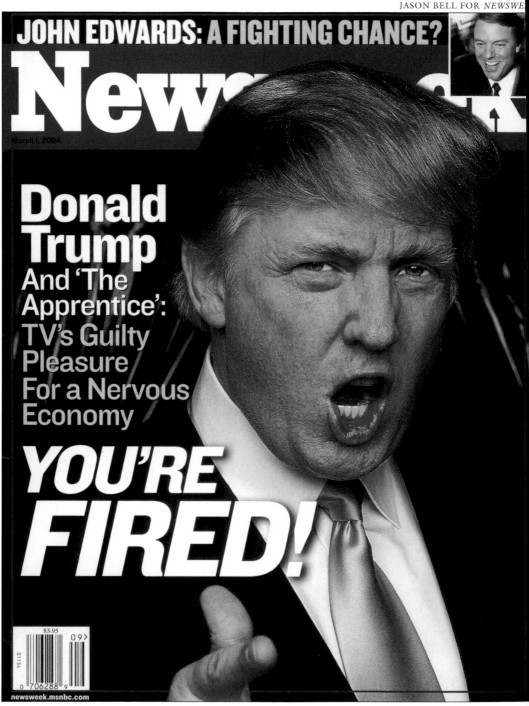

JASON BELL FOR *NEWSWE*

JOHN EDWARDS: A FIGHTING CHANCE?

New

March 1, 2004

Donald
Trump
And 'The
Apprentice':
TV's Guilty
Pleasure
For a Nervous
Economy

YOU'RE
FIRED!

$3.95

09>

0 706288 9

newsweek.msnbc.com

Newsweek *cover of March 1, 2004, with my now famous slogan.*

My gorgeous fiancée, Melania Knauss.

Tiffany and I make our entrance.

*With Tiffany, Don, Jr., and Vanessa Haydon,
at the Miss USA Pageant in Los Angeles.*

Ivanka and her friend Lysandra Ohrstrom.

Don, Jr., and Vanessa Haydon.

My youngest son, Eric, with his catch of the day.

With Darrell Hammond on the Saturday Night Live *set.*
Darrell writes: "Donald—thanks for making me look good!"

My photo from the Saturday Night Live *hall of fame.*

How to Plan for Retirement

Aging is the absolute pits. I hate it. There's nothing good about it. But there's nothing any of us can do. We all have a credit card that's been given to us by God, but that credit card has an expiration date that's fixed and firm. If we don't use that credit card properly, we have no one to blame but ourselves.

Part of aging, unfortunately, is planning for retirement. Social Security is in big trouble, and anyone who's relying on it to get them through retirement is in bigger trouble than Social Security itself. You need to plan ahead; otherwise, getting older will be all the more miserable.

There are many smart, inexpensive ways to save for retirement. As your retirement draws closer, put together an annual budget and try to determine if there are any areas in your spending where you could trim the fat. Directing more and more of your discretionary income into savings is the first step.

If you're still working, make sure to take advantage of your employer's retirement planning options. Every worker should have a 401(k) plan, and if your company does not provide one, demand it. The 401(k) allows you to take a portion of your pretax income (up to

$13,000 in deferrals per year, for most employees) and set it aside in a retirement account. It's beautiful. You lower your taxable income (and possibly your tax rate), and the government is essentially giving you money to save. There are no excuses for not participating in a 401(k). The earlier, the better. You should also make yearly contributions to a Roth IRA, an account funded by post-tax income but sheltered from capital gains taxes later down the road.

Also, study all of your existing assets to make sure that the current mix meets your near- and longer-term goals. For example, do you have too much money in stocks, or do you own multiple homes? If so, move money away from stocks and convert more and more of your holdings to safer, more liquid assets.

Once you have streamlined your investments and carefully evaluated your current budget, set up an investment and expenditure strategy to cover your remaining life. You can allocate your portfolio according to both the time frame and the amount of risk you are willing to shoulder. Bonds, CDs, and Treasury bills become the most appropriate investment vehicles for retirees or those facing retirement.

If you plan carefully (and from as young an age as possible), your retirement should be everything it's meant to be. But while you may have pulled away from work, one area you can never stop working on in life is your money. In fact, retirees need to work extra hard to guarantee that they will be solvent and financially secure until death comes a-knockin'.

How to Plan Your Estate

We're all going to die. Money can't stop that. In fact, money can't do anything about it. One thing you'll need to do is plan how your money will live on after you're long gone.

People often criticize me, saying that my success is due to the financial gifts my father passed down to me. That's absolutely untrue. It's true that I owe everything to my father, but not because of the money he gave me—it's because of the education and the practical skills he imparted to me. I plan to do the same for my children, but I absolutely refuse to allow them to live solely off inheritance. They have to make their own way in the world, and they're well aware of that.

Few activities in life match the thrill of creating wealth from one's own labors and then putting that wealth to work to seek out new challenges. Conversely, there is little in life more unrewarding than wealth that consumes its owner or sits idle and unproductive. It's my feeling that dumping huge amounts of money on your children without properly educating them about how to put that money to work—or how to make money on their own—is the worst thing a parent can do. It's negligent.

I have many friends who, through brilliance, accident of birth, or just dumb luck, have achieved great wealth. But in my dealings with them, I often come away with the distinct feeling that their wealth is more of a yoke around their necks than a benefit. They often seem to lack the courage, determination, and perhaps the talent to, on the one hand, put their wealth to work for them and, on the other hand, use the money they have actively and responsibly.

For me, wealth should not be treated as a precious work of art to be hung on a wall and admired from time to time or locked away in a vault. Rather, for me, wealth is a vehicle with which to achieve clearly defined goals. My wealth is in a perpetual kinetic state. I use it as a tool to fix what in my many business ventures may need fixing and to create new opportunities, new challenges, and, when I do it right (which, I am delighted to say, seems to be most of the time), additional wealth.

But as much as I enjoy making money, wealth carries significant social responsibility. Although my businesses and properties employ thousands of people and therefore inherently benefit society through the incomes my employees earn, I believe that some portion of personal wealth must also be used to help those who are in need, to reward good work, and to encourage better work and higher productivity in the greater community. In that way, we all benefit.

So, when planning your estate, you have two responsibilities (three, if you consider the coffers of Uncle Sam to be your "responsibility"):

1. Not to burden your children with undeserved wealth that could paralyze them, preventing them from working hard and achieving their own measures of success
2. To make a legacy for yourself that revolves around charitable giving

You should consult a lawyer who specializes in estate planning. That lawyer will take you through the legalistic and tax concerns that will empower your estate to do the most good. Then the rest is up to you.

Sit down, with your spouse if appropriate, and draw up a list of priorities. How much do your children need or deserve? Are there members of your extended family who could benefit from a gift from you? Should your bequests be tied to certain benchmarks or limited to certain uses? Which charities do you regard as worthy?

Your estate should be the last great business deal you make. Think of your estate as an investment in the future—a future that hopefully you'll be watching from up in the clouds. Make sure that whatever choices you make, you'll be seeing the greatest return on your investment. Part of thinking like a billionaire is thinking about those billions when you'll be gone.

PART III

The
Business
of Life

Whether you're a homemaker or a schoolteacher, a lawyer or a doctor, a news anchor or an aerobics instructor, you are conducting business each and every day. There's no such thing as *personal* and *work* business; it's simply your business, twenty-four hours per day. You are your own storefront, your own manager, and your own brand, so don't screw it up by making bad business decisions in life.

Don't ask other people questions you should be asking yourself. Billionaires think for themselves, stopping to review themselves and to check their motivations at each step of the way. We've all seen on *The Apprentice* that the sixteen contestants wanted to learn something. They wanted a mentor. There is nothing wrong with that, but a mentor's job is to teach someone to be independent and to learn to think that way as well. Sometimes getting the boot can be both the lesson and a boost in the right direction. But it will save time if you can go for your own blind spot before someone else gets to it first.

If you want the best, you'd better *be* the best—in all aspects of business.

How to Love Your Job

Billionaires love their jobs—not because their jobs make them wealthy, but because they wouldn't have become so wealthy doing something that they hated. You have to love what you're doing, because then it won't seem like work to you and you will bring the necessary energy to profit from it. That passion alone will take care of ninety percent of any problems with any job.

Here's another trick: Always pretend that you're working for yourself. You'll do a wonderful job in that case. It's simple, but it works. If you're finding that you don't love your job or that you're not doing a good job, demand a meeting with your boss immediately. If the situation doesn't improve, fire yourself (and your boss) and go do something else.

I never want someone working for me who doesn't want to be there, and in the same way, you shouldn't want to be there, either. Life's too short and work's too important to stick around in a situation that isn't working.

While you should strive to love your job, you should always expect the shit to hit the fan every day. It will prepare you in the best way to face every business day, and it will also keep you on your game.

Once you know you love your job, never stop and never give up. If you have a concrete wall in front of you, you must go through it. Life is difficult no matter what, but hard work and perseverance make it a lot easier.

How to Promote Yourself

I'm always amazed when people tell me I'm a master promoter. I've never thought of myself as a good promoter. I think people get confused. They think I'm successful because I'm a great promoter rather than the reverse, which is that I am successful, and a certain amount of fame has stemmed from that. I get a lot of promotional credit because my buildings are the best. The buildings make me a good promoter, not the other way around.

Promotion comes naturally from doing what you're good at. I'm good at building buildings, and that's how I promote myself—as the best builder of buildings. And everyone agrees. Neil Ostergren, a great guy who used to run the Hospitality Sales and Marketing Association, polled bigwigs in business to see what names came to mind when they thought of real estate. Mine easily came out on top.

I'm not a fan of promoting yourself, but I do think it's important to promote an image of yourself each and every day. It's part of having a sense of self and a sense of purpose. Without a sense of self or a sense of purpose, you can never think like a billionaire. So if you're good at something—and it doesn't matter what that something is (it could be tap dancing or palm reading, for all I care)—people will recognize you for it. And then people will come to you to promote you, not the other way around. Don't worry about actively promoting yourself. If you deserve to be promoted, you will be.

How to Behave
in a Meeting

In meetings you have to be innovative and break things up. Otherwise, meetings will slowly kill you with time. I can't stand long, pointless meetings. I need people to be concise because I always have about a thousand better things I could be doing with my time. Nothing stifles creativity more—and thus, good business more—than long agendas and endless rigmarole. Meetings, like all business matters, require a certain sense of hustle.

In the 1990s I remember a meeting in the big boardroom with bankers, lawyers, and members of my team, and it was late at night. We were trying to work some things out, and things weren't exactly great for me financially at that time. I looked around the room and saw a group of tired guys with their ties loosened and their sleeves rolled up, drinking coffee, and trying to keep going.

Instead of letting the meeting drag on into the night, I decided to jump ahead a few years. I started talking about the new deals I would soon be involved in. At first I received bewildered looks from everyone, but then the heaviness dissipated and we all got a fresh start with the meeting. That's an example of looking at the solution, not the problem, and it works.

Whether you're in a meeting taking notes or running it, your behavior should be at all times attuned to the matter at hand. Grandstanding or talking just to hear yourself talk are counterproductive and bound to get you fired. You should have an agenda—even if it's just in the back of your own head—and be prepared to gather and spread the necessary information in as short a time as possible. Idle chatter and banter are appropriate during the first few minutes, but after that, you're wasting everyone's time.

When you're at a meeting, monitor your behavior and work at being an observer—of yourself and of others. Try not to get angry, unless it's absolutely necessary or uncontrollable. Anger often indicates a lack of intelligence. I can remember when things could get under my skin, and when I look back, it was because I didn't have the intelligence to see them for what they were as quickly as I can now. Pay attention to your anger: Sometimes it's warranted, and sometimes it will only get in the way.

How to Organize
Your Office

I don't keep a particularly neat office, because I have so many things going on at once. I have an enormous desk and a big round table, and both are usually covered with current projects that need my attention. There is order to the apparent chaos, however, and I'd rather be effective than just tidy.

One journalist recently spent an afternoon at the Trump Organization in Trump Tower, and he commented that most of the offices were messy, but he also noticed that the teamwork was impressive, as was the energy level. We get a lot accomplished every day, and that's our bottom line. So it's not about how you organize your office but how you organize the team who works in and around that office.

How to Dress and Groom for Work

Always remember: Dress for the job you want, not the job you have. I can't stand to see the way some people dress for work these days. It's criminal. If anyone comes into my office in sneakers, or ripped clothing, or attire that looks like it belongs in a nightclub, I just can't take him or her seriously. People want to do business with people who look good, and if you look like crap, you're not going anywhere.

Clothes make the man and the woman, and if you want to be successful in life, you should start with your wardrobe. Clothing does not have to cost a fortune, but you should invest in some high-quality items that you can rotate throughout your week. It takes money to make money, and clothing is always a good investment.

People these days groom themselves even worse than they dress: dirty fingernails, stained clothing, bad breath, bad haircuts, scuffed shoes, and out-of-control facial hair. Good grooming doesn't cost money; it just costs you a little time each day. You need to check yourself in the mirror to make sure you're proud of what you're seeing there. If you appear unkempt, your business will be unkempt, too.

People ask me what happened to my signature red power ties. Nothing. I still have them; I just like going the gamut now. After I wore red ties, I noticed that everyone else started to wear them, too. I also happen to be a little superstitious. For example, I had been thinking that red ties brought me luck, so I kept wearing them. Then one day when I was wearing a big, bright red tie, I got creamed in a court decision. After that, I decided no more red ties for a while. I've joined the color spectrum, and I'm glad I did.

How to Balance Work and Pleasure

If, during the workweek, all you can think about is how many hours and minutes there are until the weekend, you'll never be a billionaire. You'll never even be a millionaire, most likely. Billionaires never wish away the minutes; life's just too good to wish it away. I hate the phrase "TGIF," and if you want to think like me, you should hate it, too.

Sometimes my weekends are even busier than my Monday-to-Friday routine. I often get some of my best work done during the weekends, when the phones die down and the fax machine stops whirring. For instance, a couple of weekends ago I carried the Olympic torch in New York City for a portion of its route as it traveled to Athens. It was an incredible honor to be a part of such an amazing tradition, and I'm proud of all the work New York City is doing currently to bring the Olympics here in 2012. That same day I also had to do three shoots for *The Apprentice* and attend a black-tie event—all on a Saturday. In between all of that activity, I managed to review some updates on my properties and make several important phone calls. I know some of those things sound like good fun—and they were—but they're also work, and I remain as committed to my job on the weekend as I do on a weekday.

Success requires work seven days per week. If you're interested in balancing work and pleasure, stop trying to balance them. Instead, make your work more pleasurable. For billionaires, work and pleasure are one and the same. Even when I'm golfing, a hobby that gives me immeasurable pleasure, I'm studying the course. If it's my own course, I'm looking for ways to improve it, and if I'm playing as a guest on another course, I'm looking for ideas and inspiration that I can adopt and use as my own.

How to Balance Work and Romance

Believe it or not, I'm a romantic guy. If there isn't any romance in my life, then I don't have much incentive to be the best that I can be. That's one reason I love women. They're great motivators. I think any honest man would agree. Romantic pursuits should motivate you to be the best, to keep growing and learning. They should be the basis from which you make a lot of your decisions in life.

So when it comes to balancing work and romance, I'm not a believer. There should be no balance. Romance should simply propel you to work harder. To me, work is as important as breathing; it's something I do automatically. I have an inherent work ethic that will never diminish. In the same way, my love for women—especially Melania—is an inherent part of me and the work that I do.

These two hungers, for work and for romance, work together in successful people. To me, both are full-out endeavors, endeavors that depend on each other and should never get in the way of one another. I give to both everything I've got, and the effort, in the long run, is always worth it.

How to Impress Anyone in Business

Here are some time-tested rules for anyone working in business that will help you impress people and thus make money:

1. Be on time. Punctuality is essential. You should never tolerate late arrivals and missed deadlines for yourself or from anyone else.
2. Do your homework. Wasting other people's time due to poor planning and thoughtlessness will only leave a *bad* impression.
3. Make a mental dossier on people. Before meeting people for the first time, do some research on them. People will be flattered if you reference a deal you know they've done or a charity they're involved in.
4. Remember people's names and small details about them. Use both in conversation. People love to hear their names and their stories said out loud.
5. Be honest. Most people can smell a lie and will appreciate honesty, even if it's not exactly what they want to be hearing.
6. Let other people talk. Any business conversation should be two-sided.

7. Be self-deprecating and disarming. Don't be a bulldozer in business; save your hardest edge for when you need it most.

Some people might think billionaires don't have to impress anyone, but most of us still live by these rules. Your manners, like your money, need to be maintained at all times.

How to Balance Money and Marriage

Don't let anyone do major surgery on your wallet. In other words, get a prenup. "M" may be for "money," but "DJT" is for prenuptial agreements. Oftentimes lawyers will recommend against a prenup because they'll be able to get a lot more money later on if you don't have one.

Everyone goes into a marriage thinking that it will last forever. But over fifty percent of the time, marriages don't work out. And when there's money and real estate and stocks and lots of personal possessions involved, it can get messy—fast! Tremendous bitter battles. A lot of my friends have gone through terrible divorces, and they always say that divorce can be the worst business deal imaginable. And I'm not just talking about men; women can be equally ruined financially without a prenup. There's nothing romantic or beautiful about a prenup, but it's better than having a sleazy lawyer do it for you or dealing with endless court proceedings. I've had two prenups, and without them I probably wouldn't be writing a book about thinking like a billionaire today.

Business is complicated and so are relationships, so the best way to avoid chaos is to have a prenuptial agreement. It's common sense. You should never ignore the power that money has to destroy relationships.

It is often the glue that brings people together and likewise the wedge that can drive them apart. Work with a lawyer to draft a prenup that will protect both you and your spouse-to-be.

People who don't agree with me should take a close look at the dynamics of a couple who experience a shift in power due to money. Both men and women, but men in particular, often struggle to adjust to situations where the woman earns more than the man does. It might be about pride, or control, or ego. It can be a difficult adjustment, even with couples who proclaim to be equals in all aspects of life. Many relationships crumble in this scenario.

Talking about money in a relationship is important, because taking care of your finances is equal to taking care of your health. It has to do with your well-being as people and as a couple. I've heard people say, "Oh, we don't talk about money," as if it's a swear word or something. This stigma is asinine. It's like enjoying being illiterate. Your financial statement is your report card. If you've worked hard for an A, don't let anyone downgrade your mark to a D for dumbbell. That's my advice.

How to Be Married

A good marriage is like negotiating an important deal: You have to consider all the factors, thoughtfully and thoroughly. If you were investing a large part of yourself and your fortune into a venture, believe me, you'd make sure you thought about it for a long time first. That's how I see marriage. It's serious, and it's important. I don't approach it any more haphazardly than I do a very important deal. In fact, considering the amount of deals I've made compared to the number of marriages I've had, I'd say I'm quite cautious about marriage. You should be, too.

I'm a bit older and certainly wiser now, and marrying Melania is a big decision, but not at all surprising. We have gotten along very well for some years now, and the comfort zone is definitely there, and we also have a lot of fun together. Enjoying someone's company is a big step in the right direction for marriage, and even though that sounds obvious, I've seen some slam-bang rotten marriages take place between two people who simply don't enjoy each other's company.

I believe strongly in the concept of "the woman behind the man," or vice versa. I have been with Melania for five years, and they have been the best five years of my life, not only personally but in business—

I am the biggest and best developer in New York; my show, *The Apprentice*, went to number one and was nominated for four Emmys; my book *How to Get Rich* became the number one business book of the year (by far); my ninety-second-a-day radio show became the number one biggest launch of a new show in the history of radio (over three hundred stations), and so on. So I figured I better marry the woman who stood behind me (and in front of me) during this amazing and crazy period—and fast!

How to Make Good Friends

First, have something in common. I am good friends with Regis Philbin because he is a positive guy, and therefore I always enjoy his company. I, too, am a positive type of guy, and I prefer to see the good things in life, so we have a great time together. That's one recipe for a good friendship: simple and solid.

Consider my friendship with Richard LeFrak. He called me the other day when I was in the middle of an important meeting, but he's too good a friend for me not to take his call. He's just the best of the best. We were joking around together, and I told him that I was looking out for him because I was keeping an eye on some scaffolding work being done on his building that I can see from my office windows. If the workers start slacking or the work looks shoddy, you can bet I'll be dialing Richard in a second—and he would expect me to.

We spoke for a couple more minutes; he asked about my shooting schedule for *The Apprentice,* and I asked about his health. He asked me about my children, and I asked after his. He has two amazing sons, and one of them, Harry, is a true dynamo who will go on to great heights. Attending to that sort of detail is necessary to maintain good friendships. You have to *invest* yourself in the details of your friends' lives. Otherwise, there's just no bond between you.

And then there's the old saying "To have a friend, be a friend." Well, sometimes. I've been around some selfish people, and their idea of a friend is for you to be everything they want you to be. The minute you step out of the role they've designed for you, watch out! You're a bad friend!

It helps if your friends have a level of confidence equal to yours, which will eradicate any envy or jealousy they might otherwise have. I am a successful man, and I've seen a lot of ill-concealed envy toward me because of my accomplishments. I quickly have to assess those who are sincere and those who aren't because I've met so many of the latter. It's not a condemnation but a part of human nature that I'm well aware of by now.

Steve Wynn, the successful Las Vegas hotel impresario, is a friend. We have had some tremendous ups and downs with each other, but somehow it seems to work, and we always seem to end up together. Steve called me when he was thinking of changing the name of his hotel in Las Vegas (which will be a great success, by the way) from Le Reve to Wynn. I told him to do it. Now we are both fighting HBO, using the same lawyer, Barry Langberg, as HBO is attempting to do an awful movie on a battle we had in Atlantic City. I hope HBO will be smart enough to make corrections before a lot of money is spent doing battle over it.

I know many successful people who only want to be with people who are not successful—it makes them feel better about themselves. I have one very successful and well-known friend who boasts loudly that he will only hang out with losers. (How would you like to be one of them?) I, on the other hand, don't discriminate—I like (and dislike) all sorts of people—winners, losers, and those in the middle!

How to Know Whether Someone Is Loyal

It's taken me a long time to figure out how to recognize whether someone's loyal or not. I suppose it takes some bad mistakes to learn this valuable lesson. I'm not sure it can be taught. These days, I have a better sense of people and their motivations, and most of my friends and colleagues have proved loyal to me.

A lot of people envy billionaires and successful people, so I have to be mindful of that every time I approach a new relationship. The people in my life who recognize the high price I have paid to be where I am—in stress, in hard work, and even in failure—are the loyal ones. I always try to surround myself with people who would stand by me if tomorrow I woke up a pauper.

The best time to test whether or not somebody is loyal is when things are going horribly for you. When I was having trouble in the early nineties, I learned a lot about loyalty because there were people I thought would be totally loyal to me who weren't. And then, of course, there were people I thought would be disloyal, and they were great. When you're successful, people will kiss your ass and clamber to be around you. When things aren't going so well, loyalty and disloyalty surface naturally. I don't like to test people, and I've learned that people will prove themselves to be what they are sooner or later.

By the way, almost all of the people who were not loyal to me in the early nineties have called me since then to try to get together. My response to them is very simple: F____ you! One thing I have learned in life is that if someone is disloyal to you once, they will be disloyal to you again.

I had a friend in New York who would call me all the time and who was a lot of fun to be with. He is a very successful businessman (I think!). After years of being his friend and doing him favors, a problem came up for me that he was in a position to solve easily. He claimed that he didn't have the power over the situation that I thought he had (which was nonsense) and did not come through for me. I believe he didn't even try very hard. Needless to say, he is no longer a friend.

Stuff

Billionaires are not defined simply by the size of their holdings but also by the quality of their stuff. There's no point in being a billionaire if you cannot enjoy those billions.

To have the best, you have to know the best. Thinking like a billionaire means recognizing the best and enjoying the best. Of course, it takes practice. Can you confidently name the top five jewelers in the world? The best champagne? The best, most exclusive real estate? The most highly rated restaurants? The top art dealers? If not, you've got a long way to go to be a billionaire. But don't feel bad, because I don't know all the answers—other than the real estate ones—either!

It's nice that people think Dom Perignon is a good champagne, because it is. But it isn't the best. When I hear people bragging about drinking it, it's an automatic tip-off that they're not clued in. Always remember that the most famous doesn't always equal the best.

The best is a quest. Elevate your tastes; don't stagnate in the mediocre-to-good category. It will end up categorizing you. If an expert were to review your pantry or your wardrobe or your travel itineraries, how do you think you'd rate? How can you aim for the best if you don't know what you're aiming for? But at the same time, always remember that some of the richest and most successful people, like Warren Buffett (or, before his death, the great Sam Walton), live very simple lives. Sam drove to work in an old Chevrolet every day—I love it!

If you want to truly *be* rich, recognize the virtue of making your own choices versus doing what is expected or what everyone else is doing. If wine makes you ill, don't drink it just because you think it makes you seem sophisticated or worldly. That's preposterous. If you do like wine, learn about it, and if you don't, find something else to spend your money on. I often see people who supposedly love wine making stupid choices. It's a giveaway that they don't know what they're doing, and on several levels. Much as we don't like to admit it, we are often judged by our choices, even minor ones.

Luxury is what takes us from the ordinary to the extraordinary. Here's a Donald Trump "consumer guide" for the best luxuries around:

The Best Car: My favorite car is a Mercedes. I've had one for a long time, and it's reliable, elegant, and sturdy all at once. I have no complaints about my Mercedes. It's never disappointed me. The cars are not temperamental, and they make my life easier. Mercedes cars are also great because they are classy without being ostentatious. I also have a Ferrari, a Lamborghini, and a bunch of other cars in different places.

The Best Suit: I wear Brioni suits, which I buy off the rack. Some people think it's best to have custom-tailored clothing. I don't recommend it unless you have an oddly shaped body, and unless you have a great deal of time.

The Best Cuff Links: The best cuff links are the TRUMP five-star diamond cuff links that Joe Cinque of the Five Star Diamond Awards gave to me. I keep some on hand to give to people as gifts, and they are great-looking. I also wear solid gold cuff links from time to time, but I have to say, I prefer Joe's TRUMP cuff links.

The Best Shirts: I've worn some great shirts over the years, but I now favor Brioni (the same brand as my favorite suits). Brioni shirts are fitted so they feel and look great. I used to have a favorite dry cleaner, located in Atlantic City, but I've mellowed a bit and I can handle the dry cleaners in New York City just fine now. Actually, once you get a good shirt, who really notices anyway?

The Best Ties: Brioni and Hermès make the best ties. And I must say, as I keep mentioning Brioni, that they graciously supply me with my clothing for *The Apprentice.*

The Best Shoes: I love a variety of high-end shoes. I can remember when I thought some good shoes were great until I found some *really* great shoes. The price was substantially greater, too, but after wearing them, I can't go back to the others. I also find that they last for a much longer period of time, so that the real cost is actually less.

The Best Jewelry: I go to Graff, Harry Winston, Asprey, Tiffany, and Fred Leighton for jewelry. Asprey has been around since the eighteenth century, and their jewelry makes the most beautiful woman look even better. In addition to gems, Asprey is also famous for their silver, leather, porcelain, and crystal. Asprey's flagship store is in the Trump Tower, so I can slip in there whenever I want, almost always to buy something for Melania. You can buy a gift for anyone there, and the salespeople are excellent. Winston and Graff have, I believe, the best diamonds in the world.

The Best Golf Equipment: If you're new to the game, you don't have to invest a lot of money to buy a decent set of clubs. Cary

Stephan, the golf pro at the Trump National Golf Club, tells me that only good golfers can tell the difference between good and bad clubs. It is important to buy a set of clubs designed with your frame and your weight in mind. Seniors need different clubs than juniors, men need different clubs than women, and so on.

If you're a decent golfer, definitely go for the modern technology. Get every advantage you can. The new equipment totally outperforms the old stuff. I have always liked Callaway, while Lee Rinker, head professional at Trump International Golf Club in Palm Beach, prefers TaylorMade. Good players can use forged irons, but the average person should use a perimeter-weighted iron. Also, make sure the shaft flex matches your swing speed.

The newest balls, particularly the ones made by Titleist and Callaway, are fantastic as well. These balls go forever when hit off a tee but still have great feel in the short game. It's like having two balls for the price of one.

The Best Furniture: The best furniture doesn't have a brand name. Furniture is as diverse as it comes, but I've noticed the brand names aren't consistent to one level of quality or taste. I never like all the pieces by one designer, and sometimes I'll find one incredible piece in a collection that otherwise leaves me uninspired. That's why I take so long to decide about certain pieces. One badly chosen item can ruin an entire room. Furniture is as important as lighting to a room, about which I'm equally demanding.

I admire Mies van der Rohe very much, but I don't like sitting in his chairs. Furniture should be elegant, but it also needs to be comfortable. Whoever or whatever manufacturer can provide that combination will get my business.

The Best Antiques: These come from high-end antique dealers. Collecting antiques is up there with collecting art, and I go for the most reputable dealer I can find. Sometimes there's a fine line between good-looking junk and the real thing, and a dealer will spare you wasted time and scams.

The Best Credit Card: The best credit cards are Visa and American Express. I even did a commercial for Visa, and American Express is a great tenant of mine at 40 Wall Street.

The Best Shampoo: The best shampoo is Head & Shoulders.

The Best Book: I have two: *The Art of the Deal* and *How to Get Rich,* both by Donald J. Trump.

The Best Movie: My favorite movie of all time is *Citizen Kane.*

The Best Album: There's so much great music. For me, I'd have to say it's a toss-up between Frank Sinatra, Tony Bennett, and Elton John. I never get tired of listening to them and probably never will. Frank Sinatra's favorite singer was Tony Bennett, so those two sort of go together. Any album by any of them is bound to be fantastic. And besides that, Tony lives in one of my buildings.

In Trump Tower, we play a variety of music—anything from renditions of "Moon River" to versions of Rachmaninoff's famous piano concertos. Some people call it cheesy, but others love it, and so do I. If you love a certain kind of music, don't let other people's tastes influence your own. Whatever's the best for you is the best. Never forget that. And by the way, I also love Eminem.

The Best Broadway Show: My favorite Broadway show is *Evita* by Andrew Lloyd Webber, starring Patti LuPone. I saw it six times, mostly with Ivana. *Evita* is not on Broadway right now, but I'm hopeful that they'll bring it back. Also, *The Phantom of the Opera* was great!

The Best Painting: The best painting is the finger painting of a house by my daughter Tiffany. Nothing else comes close.

The Best Ice Cream: Cherry Vanilla by Häagen-Dazs is by far my favorite flavor, and I've tried a lot of them, as I'm an ice-cream fan from way back. When I open my own ice-cream parlor in Trump Tower, maybe we'll give Häagen-Dazs a run for its money.

The Best Hamburger: I have two answers for this one. I like McDonald's hamburgers and the DT Burger as served at the Trump Grill in Trump Tower. The DT Burger is definitely more deluxe, but I've been a loyal McDonald's customer and even did a major ad for them.

Places

Billionaires tend to be well traveled and cultured. You should be, too. There's no excuse for staying home; the world's too fantastic to miss out on it. I wish I could travel more, but I am having too much fun at home. When you do decide to travel, always pack the word "elite." It's a great word. It's a great place to be, too. If you want to think like a billionaire, elite should never be a destination that's too far away. But don't confuse "elite" with "expensive." Elite is much more about a frame of mind, about curiosity and experience and appetite. Even if you haven't got tons of money yet, why not prepare yourself for when you do?

How to Travel in Style
Even If You Don't Have
Your Own Jet

You don't need your own jet or your own yacht to travel in style. Traveling in style usually takes cash—lots of it. But beyond cash, traveling in style requires a certain mind-set—a mind-set that you can develop for free.

The first trick is to go to places where you will be comfortable. It's impossible to travel in style if you're fearing for your life, or the temperature is unbearable, or you can't eat anything because it will all make you sick. Don't run off to crummy places because you've found a good deal. One day in the south of France will be far more restive and rewarding than a whole summer spent in a hellhole. Use your head when making travel plans. It's okay to look for a good deal, but you sometimes have to spend money to enjoy yourself. Not to do so is a waste of money and can be dangerous.

I make a habit of only traveling to places with running water and good amenities. I don't have a calling to the great outdoors, unlike both of my sons. I've never felt I needed to climb mountains or ride rapids down a river. Why try to climb Mount Everest when you can see it perfectly well on television or in a book? I always say, "Don't challenge nature, because ultimately, nature will win." You're far better off in a hotel.

So while I'm not an expert in off-road, rugged travel, I know what I'm talking about when it comes to hotels and resorts. Here are some tips for when you travel—and when you want to travel like I do:

1. Never check your luggage. That's a cardinal rule. Checked luggage is lost luggage. If you have an important meeting, you will not have time to shop for a new set of clothing.

2. Stay in a nice hotel. People's perception of you is influenced by the quality of the hotel you're staying in. If you're trying to sell yourself or your business, others will not perceive you as a deal maker if you're staying at the Fleabag Inn.

3. Get your suits pressed. It should be one of the first things you do after you arrive at your hotel. Most hotels will offer complimentary pressing, so there's no excuse for leaving a hotel looking like your suit's been crumpled in the bottom of a suitcase for days.

4. Bring golf clothing. You never know when you'll be called upon for an impromptu round of golf. You can rent clubs, but clothing and shoes that fit are harder to come by.

5. Always arrange your transportation from the airport to your hotel before your plane takes off. You can waste a lot of time and money stuck at the airport with a beat-up taxi as your only option. Plan ahead.

6. Have your assistant call the hotel in advance to let the manager know of your arrival. Good managers at good hotels know the comings and goings of each guest, and if they are alerted to your arrival, you're bound to get better service.

How to Be Treated Like Royalty in a Hotel

The best way to be treated like royalty in a hotel is to tip well. Tip the bellhop who brings up your luggage, tip the concierge when he or she makes your restaurant reservation, and tip the waitstaff when they deliver your room service. If you tip liberally, the hotel workers will watch your back. When you need a reservation at the best restaurant to impress a client or you need a car five minutes ago, hotel workers will absolutely bend over backward for you if they know that you'll take care of them.

The best way to judge a hotel is on cleanliness. That's huge. If you walk into a hotel room and it's dirty, check out. Run, actually. A hotel's rooms should be immaculate. If you've taken my advice and opted for a top-notch hotel, you're paying top dollar for what should be top service, so never tolerate mess or filth.

Veterans of hotels always know to ask for an upgrade and always know to negotiate their rates. You might get one or the other, and there's no shame in trying; there's shame only in not doing so. If you're staying multiple nights or over a weekend, your chances of an upgrade or a rate reduction are even greater.

If you get to your room and you hate what you find, complain. Don't be shy. Ask for the manager (don't complain directly to the bellhop), and I assure you that he or she will try his or her best to help you. You could get a new room or an upgrade. If the hotel's booked, you might be able to get the price reduced. Too many people are too shy to complain. Neither you nor the hotel staff members want your stay to be unpleasant.

And finally, expect the staff to be pleasant, smiling, and aggressively hospitable. You can be grumpy and tired, especially if you've just come off a red-eye flight or out of a long meeting, but the staff should be as accommodating and as polite as possible. If not, you're at the wrong hotel.

How to Get the Best Service at a Restaurant

Get to know the restaurant's owner, the maitre d', the waiters, and anyone else associated with the restaurant. Some of my favorite people in New York are restaurateurs: Jean-Georges Vongerichten, who's the genius behind Jean Georges in the Trump International Hotel; Sirio Maccioni, who runs Le Cirque; and Giuseppe Cipriani. I know how demanding they are of themselves as far as quality and innovation go. They're artists and craftsmen when it comes to cooking and hospitality. There are only a few people in the world in their league. And they never let a customer down. There are a lot of traditional businessmen in New York who could learn a lot about business from watching Sirio, Jean-Georges, and Giuseppe.

If you can't afford the best restaurants, the same advice works anywhere. I'm building a golf course in Bedminster, New Jersey, and whenever I'm there, I always try to visit Bedminster Pizza. It's about three minutes away from the golf club, and it's the best pizza I've ever had. The men who work there, some of whom barely speak English, treat me like a king. Great service is available at every level of the food chain. You just need to know how to find it.

Another trick is to treat the waiters and the restaurant owners as you would treat the host of a dinner or a party. Always remember that even though you may be paying for your meal, you're still a guest of the restaurant. If you act like a guest, you'll be treated like one— sometimes like the guest of honor.

How to Improve Your Golf Game

If you play a lot of golf, your game will improve with time. Cary Stephan, the golf pro at the Trump National Golf Club in Briarcliff Manor, New York, feels that good golfers need to put in two to three hours per week of practice—whether it's on the putting green, or playing rounds, or at the driving range. Serious golfers looking to improve their game should also devote an hour a week to instruction. Golf, like everything else in life, requires dedication.

The rest is pure talent. I recently played golf with Annika Sorenstam, the Swedish golf champion, at the Trump National Golf Club at Briarcliff Manor. Hard as I try to be fair about the fairer sex, I still don't like being outdriven by a woman. After playing with Annika, I have to say that I'm happy I'm in the real estate business. I did, however, ask her how she does what she does so well. Her answer reminded me of Babe Ruth's: "I just do it." Basically, she works hard, but she's got great talent.

I was recently asked whether I see golf as a business or as a pleasure. I had to say that I find even more pleasure in building great golf courses than in playing the game. There is something so aesthetically pleasing about bringing a golf course to life. In fact, I feel guilty now if I'm playing golf at Winged Foot, which is a great course, because if I'm playing there, it's for pleasure only, not business. On my own courses, I can play and work at the same time, as I'm scouting the course for any problems I might see or possible improvements to make. I'm doing two things at once that way.

How to Find
Great Vacation Resorts

To zero in on a great vacation resort, ask people where they've been lately and ask for a firsthand account. Joe Cinque travels constantly, and he always gives me an honest opinion of where and what's the best. If he speaks highly of a place, I put it on my mental list of destinations. Sometimes I'll flip through magazine articles and photographs, especially a beautiful publication such as *Elite Traveler.* I know that Douglas Gollan, the president and editor in chief, does a lot of the research himself. His tastes are sophisticated and discerning. I caught up with Doug recently at the Beverly Hills Hotel, and his immediate agenda included Dubai, South America, Geneva, Paris, and other European cities. He can always provide you with a list of the hottest destinations, as does his magazine.

But I am fortunate not to have to travel far to find one of the most beautiful places on earth, which is the Mar-a-Lago Club in Palm Beach, Florida. Melania loves it there more than anyplace, and she spent years going to the south of France, Portofino, Lake Como, and other beautiful places in Europe. She prefers Mar-a-Lago to them all, and so do I.

Etiquette

HOW TO TIP

Tipping, unless service is absolutely reprehensible, is mandatory. You should always tip waitstaff at least fifteen percent, if not twenty percent. I always make a point of tipping the maître d' or the sommelier if it's appropriate. If you make a habit of certain restaurants, you'll be increasingly less welcome and will receive shoddy service if you don't pay up.

In other aspects of daily life, tipping can confuse people, but I always say, "More is more." I know I'm an advocate for penny-pinching, but you have to think of service workers as your colleagues in the business of life. Service jobs are never easy, and service workers can be some of the more tolerant, professional, and polite people working today. Learn from them.

You should always give at least a couple of dollars (and, in some cases, a lot more) to valets, skycaps, restroom attendants, door attendants, bellhops, coat checks, the concierge, and housekeepers. If someone goes out of their way for you or makes your life easier in any way, tip them a lot more. I think a sure indication of a loser is someone who can't tip adequately.

HOW TO ATTEND A PARTY

I can remember the times when I was not invited to as many parties as I am today. Today I am overwhelmed with invitations. I'm wanted places—sometimes for five or six events per night—but I don't go to many of them.

When I was younger and less known, I avoided parties where I might be considered a fringe member of those on the invitation list. It's never a good idea to be at a party where you're not welcome, and if you are invited somewhere, don't show up too early and don't leave too late. I'm always amazed to see a party that's emptying with three or four oblivious partygoers just not wanting to leave. Also, drinking too much or behaving inappropriately is a one-way ticket to the Z-list.

If you're going to talk about something at a party, make sure you know what you're talking about. I was recently at a party where I was subjected to listening to a woman who let us know exactly how much she didn't know about owning a yacht by trying to tell everyone how much she did know about it. Unfortunately for her, quite a few of us there had owned yachts, myself included. We were polite and let it slide, but we all knew this know-it-all was trying to impress the wrong people. If she had known what she was talking about, she would have known that the second-greatest day of a man's life is the day he buys a yacht, but the *greatest* day of a man's life is the day he sells it.

HOW TO BEGIN AND END
A CONVERSATION

Interested is interesting. If you remember that simple rule, you should have no trouble making conversation. I'm gregarious by nature, but a simple key for those who are more introverted is to be curious. Ask questions that will make the other person talk. After all, most people love to hear themselves talk, so if you're shy, let the other party do the work.

Most people are fascinating if you ask the right questions, and small talk can be one of the best ways to educate yourself. Rarely does a day go by in which I don't have five to ten conversations that change the way I see the world.

You can end a conversation quickly if you don't mind being blunt. Other ways are to stop talking, move away a bit, pretend you see someone you know across the room, or just say, "Enjoy your evening. Nice talking to you." The phone is easier because you can simply hang up.

I enjoy most conversations I engage in, especially with contractors, and since I usually have a lot of people to talk to, most people are considerate and don't bog me down. Those who do will get the message, and if they don't, I just tell them I have to move on. No one enjoys being rude, but on occasion you need to be—otherwise, you'll spend your entire life trapped in pointless conversations and small talk.

HOW TO GIVE A GOOD GIFT

Never just pick something generic. It's a waste of money, and the gesture will be forgotten in a second. Strategic gift giving should be thoughtful and appropriate. It should reflect the recipient's interests or your relationship with the person. Gift giving takes time and careful planning. Don't plan on buying a gift on your way to see someone. If you're clueless when it comes to shopping, ask a trusted personal assistant or a friend to help you—especially when you're shopping for the opposite sex.

I keep up with catalogs from Bergdorf, Tiffany, Louis Vuitton, and other fine stores, so I'll know what's new and what's out there. Occasionally, as I walk through a place, I'll see something that catches my eye and will buy it on the spot.

HOW TO CORRECT SOMEONE

I'm a New Yorker, so I tell it like it is. Be up front and direct with people, and they will return the favor. But sometimes, in more sensitive social situations, you have to consider the source and let it slide.

In business and in life, I've heard people say things that are so outrageously incorrect that I don't feel it's worth my energy to say anything. Sometimes it's easy to just say, "You might want to check into that. I heard differently," and leave it at that.

If you can avoid an altercation, do so, since most of them aren't worth your time and energy. I have to set a lot of things straight every day at work, and doing this during social hours is a total turnoff. I'd rather walk away and let other people waste their time. People will, hopefully, correct themselves eventually.

HOW TO CRITICIZE SOMEONE

It's best to avoid criticizing anyone. Compliments work better, and sometimes silence is the best form of criticism available. I've known people who have said bad things to and about me who cannot take criticism themselves. Most people are one-way streets, and it's better not to spend your time dodging head-on traffic. If you stay silent, people will eventually make fools of themselves without your help at all. It's revenge the easy way.

HOW TO SAY NO

Learning how to say no is crucial to thinking like a billionaire. We are faced with a barrage of requests each and every day—for time, for money, and for favors. We have to learn to say no most of the time, occasionally to some worthy causes and some great opportunities.

When it comes to saying no in the context of a deal, I learned a valuable lesson from one of my lawyers: Distill the information presented to you. Lawyers are pros at distilling complex information, and it's a skill worth cultivating. As you read over the terms of a deal or a contract, translate the language by using the phrase "in other words . . ." and then paraphrase the rest.

You will begin to see the tricky ways in which language can be used. If you can distill the language into simpler terms, you'll be able to see how the deal will reward you and also what it will require of you. Once you have the pluses and minuses straight in your head, saying no (if necessary) will be a lot easier.

Frankly—and this advice might strike you as strange—accept it when people are not nice to you. I like it when people are not nice because they're easier to control. It's much more difficult to be tough with someone who is nice. If they're nasty, saying no is a cinch.

PART IV

Slices of the Billionaire's Life

I could continue giving you advice about how to think like a billionaire, but I've always felt that the best way to teach someone is by example. Following are some excellent examples of a billionaire's mind at work.

Columbia University

Last year I wrote a critical letter to Lee Bollinger, the president of Columbia University and the former president of the University of Michigan. As a committed real estate developer in New York City, I feel that it's my responsibility to look out for some of the cultural institutions in town, and Columbia University is one of New York City's greatest treasures. Part of Bollinger's mission is to expand the size of the university—not just its academic offerings but also its campus—and I couldn't agree with that mission more.

But it came to the attention of the real estate community that Bollinger was interested in buying up land in Harlem, the university's neighborhood. To my shock, Bollinger at that time controlled approximately forty percent of the seventeen acres he was looking for. Take a lesson from Bollinger's mistake: Never, never tip your hand about your desire to own something, particularly real estate, before you make a deal. You'll only end up paying through the nose. Bollinger will have to pay a premium on the remaining sixty percent of the property because the owners now know how much he wants it. That's simply bad business practice, and if I were on Columbia's board of trustees, I would tell Bollinger, "You're fired!"

Not only is this scenario an example of bad strategy, but Bollinger is also buying in the wrong location. Al Lerner, a close friend of mine who, sadly, passed away from cancer, was on Columbia's board for some time, and he had a fantastic vision. He thought Columbia should have occupied fifteen magnificent acres of unobstructed land from 59th to 62nd Streets fronting both West End Avenue and the Hudson River. It would have brought part of the Columbia campus into the heart of Manhattan and made the campus more accessible to New Yorkers. As it is now, Columbia is in a horrible location, and thanks to Bollinger, it will stay that way forever. Columbia deserves the best location, not the worst. By the way, I own the land that Columbia should be buying.

The United Nations Mess

Only an incompetent could create and continue the mess, or I should say *messes*, at the United Nations. Kofi Annan, the secretary general of the United Nations, has created a fiasco out of one of the world's most valuable institutions.

Let me give you some background on what's going on at the UN. Not so very long ago, I had a meeting with a high-ranking official of the United Nations regarding the possible renovation and restoration of the UN complex in New York City. After studying the details of the renovation, and with the constraint that there be no relocation of any employees during this reconstruction, I knew I could accomplish exactly what the United Nations wanted in two years and at the cost of $400 million. They had originally approached me because they could not believe I'd built Trump World Tower at the United Nations Plaza for only $300 million, but it was true. If you know what you're doing, you can get things done at the right price and the right way.

Then, without hearing from the United Nations on my proposal, I read that they had hired someone to do exactly what they had asked of me. This other party would renovate and restore the United

Nations complex but was demanding a seven-year completion schedule at the cost of $1.5 billion.

It does not take a genius to recognize the enormous difference in these proposals—several years and $1.5 billion, or $1.1 billion more than I would spend for a job that would not be as good as mine. It makes me wonder: Who is in charge at the United Nations? Could they be as incompetent in world affairs as they are at simple numbers? Does anyone else find this situation as alarming as I do?

While the fundamental premise of the United Nations is wonderful, perhaps we need to reevaluate its current function. It started out so well. What has happened? With these enormous oversights in the area of finance, perhaps we need to start worrying.

The Statue of Liberty

Paris has the Eiffel Tower, Rome has the Coliseum, and we've got the Statue of Liberty. To me, it's the icon of New York, and it moves me to see it up close, even to see photographs of it, and to think about what it symbolizes. I often imagine the boats full of immigrants who have sailed into New York Harbor with that amazing statue to greet them. It still stands proudly today.

Despite our sometimes strained political relations, we should not forget that this landmark was a gift from the country of France—the France of liberty, equality, and fraternity. The French recognized our quest as Americans and gave us this incredible symbol in appreciation for what America represents. I think that the recent divide between France and the United States is a tragedy. We would have felt as bad for them if the Eiffel Tower or La Defense had been destroyed as they felt for us when the Towers came down on September 11.

For one of the opening scenes for the second season of *The Apprentice,* Mark Burnett and his crew took me to the Statue of Liberty. As we approached Lady Liberty, I was taken back to my youth when I was told I was fortunate to be in America, that I had opportunities other people in the world could only dream about. And here

I am, a major player in the greatest city of this incredible country, and I realize once again how amazingly lucky I have been.

With the parents I had and this country as my backbone, anything was possible. I operated on that premise of possibility, and I'm walking, talking proof of the American Dream. For me, the American Dream is not just a dream; it's a reality.

Breakfast at the Waldorf

I like going to the Waldorf, especially when I'm receiving an award. Recently, the International Radio and Television Society had a breakfast for me, the casts from *Queer Eye for the Straight Guy* and *Sex and the City,* producer Michael Patrick King, Bob Schieffer of *Face the Nation,* and Herb Scannell of Nickelodeon Networks. Jeff Zucker of NBC was also there to announce that while it took five guys to save Bravo, it only took one—me—to save NBC. Then Bob Wright, chairman and CEO of NBC, took the stage to introduce me.

It was an honor to receive the award, because, as Bob Schieffer mentioned, we have a responsibility in the television and radio industry to try to make media intelligent. That's our approach with *The Apprentice,* and to be recognized for my contribution feels great. As our culture changes, so must our television, or it would lose relevance. In addition to providing entertainment, radio and television have increasingly become powerful tools for educational enlightenment. I keep this in mind for both my radio and my television programs.

As power breakfasts go, that one was up there with the best, and we all agreed to keep up the good work.

Ten Amazing Minutes

Steve Wynn recently called and told me he was about to bid on a great painting, a Vermeer. The auction was taking place at Sotheby's in London, and Steve asked me to listen in on the bidding process. It was very interesting, especially for someone like me who has never been a big buyer of paintings. Steve loves this Vermeer painting, and usually, what Steve wants, he gets.

The bidding began at $10 million and quickly escalated to $24 million when Steve entered the fray. People began to drop out, and finally, it was just Steve and one other bidder until Steve ended up winning at $30 million. It was a really amazing ten minutes, and Steve now has a painting by an artist whose work will probably never go to market again. I look forward to seeing it!

People Magazine and What People Do

Ann Moore, the chairman and CEO of Time, Inc., invited me to speak to a *People* magazine management meeting—"to share a few secrets on your leadership success," as she put it. My speaking fee is typically $250,000, but because *People* magazine has always treated me well, I decided to do Ann a favor. I opened the lunch meeting with the observation that they'd left me out of their latest issue, "The 50 Most Beautiful People," but after setting that straight, we were off to a good time.

I began by discussing the power of the media. When Jean Georges, the wonderful restaurant in the Trump International Hotel and Tower, first opened, I told chef Jean-Georges Vongerichten that I absolutely hated the interior design and didn't even want to eat there because of it. He said, "Mr. Trump, I want people to notice the food, not the decor." I thought that was one of the greatest lines of pure bullshit I'd ever heard and told him so. Then *The New York Times* wrote an absolute rave review of the food, giving the restaurant its highest rating, and suddenly, I thought the room looked pretty good after all. The newspaper's analysis and praise of the restaurant completely changed my mind. That's power.

I continue to alienate members of the press on occasion, but on the whole, I like them. I know their jobs aren't easy. That day, facing a room of attractive and attentive publishing types, I mentioned that while they may be lovely young women and sharp-looking young men, they couldn't fool me. I know they're vicious. I deal with vicious people every day, but most of the time, they *look* vicious. These people appeared well polished, but I told them I know they're out to get me. The room laughed.

The media represents great power. As someone who has received a lot of attention from the media, I know that its power to make someone recognizable is unbelievable. I had always been relatively well known, but it was nothing compared to my fame now. Even six-year-olds walk up to me on the street and shout "You're fired!," and elderly men in their Rolls-Royces in Palm Beach will roll down their windows to yell at me as they drive by. I thought I was famous before, but I was wrong. *Now* I'm famous.

In order to comply with Ann's wish that this be a business meeting, I spent a few minutes talking about success—and gave the audience some advice on how to find it for themselves. Then, as I suspected, I discovered that the only thing they were interested in was *The Apprentice*. I don't mind answering these questions, but the level of interest always surprises me.

With this crowd, however, I also asked questions about the show. What did they like about it? Should I expand my inner circle of advisers? What task pertinent to magazine publishing would they come up with for the candidates? And so forth. One person asked me what had been the biggest surprise to me about the show. I answered that the biggest surprise had been the show's success. Ninety-five percent of new TV shows don't make it. Those aren't odds I like, and it's a good thing I didn't know that going in or I never would have signed on in the first place.

As I was discussing *The Apprentice*, I also mentioned that prior to the show's success, I remembered standing with Melania behind a guy who was also waiting to get into the NBC Upfront event at Lincoln Center last year. I mentioned to Melania that he was a great-looking guy. It turned out to be Rob Lowe. He also had a new TV show coming up, and I remembered thinking that I really didn't want to go up against someone who looked like that. I'd never make it. Unfortunately, his show didn't make it, and mine made it big. So you never know what will work.

I also told the audience that I thought certain kinds of people shouldn't be on *The Apprentice,* such as Sam and Omarosa, who were loose cannons as far as I was concerned—but that's part of the entertainment factor. If we'd had sixteen intelligent, polished, and productive people from the audience as candidates, it might not have been as interesting a mix. That's what Mark Burnett and his team do so well— they put together a group in which the common denominators may be intelligence and ambition, but with enough variety to be entertaining, and maybe create some sparks along the way. Disasters can be more interesting than smooth sailing. So much for my casting instincts, but these are things we learn along the way. If it were up to me, I'd choose sixteen supermodels—not good!

I ended the conversation by bringing the topic back to business. I mentioned that whomever I choose as the winner on *The Apprentice* will always be chosen from strictly a business, not an entertainment, viewpoint. I don't want someone who is entertaining; I want someone who knows what he or she is doing. After all, my own life is entertaining enough.

In Praise of Audacity

I agreed to give a speech in New York City to seven hundred people from Sanofi-Synthelabo, Inc., a pharmaceutical company, for Patti Giles. Patti is a terrific businesswoman, and she and the Sanofi group had all been at my Mar-a-Lago Club for a dinner a few months earlier, so I wanted to welcome them to my city.

I know from experience that this group is hardworking—I had invited some of the team to play golf with me at the Trump International Golf Club in Palm Beach, and they all declined. Every single one of them turned me down! However, I realized that these people had their priorities straight. They love their work, are responsible to the positions they hold, and are completely focused.

Over the course of my speech, I told them that if you can't dream about new products, they will never happen. I also pointed out how important it is to set their own standards. That will ensure that they remain innovators in their field. I already know how disciplined they are, so I am stressing their creativity and urging them to go against the tide.

In summing up, I told them what I've said before, but these are points worth repeating if you are intent on big success:

1. Think big.
2. Stay focused.
3. Be paranoid (keep your guard up).
4. Be passionate.
5. Don't ever give up.
6. Love what you are doing.

To be a winner, you must think like a winner. Try it. You'll be surprised. And before long, you might be thinking like a billionaire.

Pageants

As the saying goes, Miss America is the girl who lives next door. Miss USA is the girl you *wished* lived next door. To diversify my investments, I entered into a partnership for ownership and broadcast rights with the NBC network for the three largest beauty competitions in the world: the Miss Universe, Miss USA, and Miss Teen USA pageants.

Few people are aware of the large audience that pageants have worldwide or of the weight they carry internationally. Their value to the economies of the countries that host them is enormous, and the bidding for them is a competitive and serious business.

While millions around the world tune in each year to see a new titleholder crowned, few people realize just what the year entails for each young woman. All three (Miss USA, Miss Universe, and Miss Teen USA) become bona fide full-time employees of the Miss Universe Organization and immediately put their lives on hold for a year to relocate to New York. They all move into a three-bedroom luxury suite in my Trump Place development.

Whether or not you enjoy beauty pageants, they serve a purpose aside from the celebration of beautiful young women. The importance of good works is at the center of the pageantry, and these women are using their gifts in incredible ways. In that sense, the pageants provide an excellent lesson for everyone. Marco de la Cruz, who works as a motivational coach in Los Angeles, told me how impressed he was with the contestants of the Miss USA pageant after working with them for a few weeks. He said that what might be perceived as a sexist or narcissistic event was much more, due to the social conscience the contestants displayed. He felt the pageant was a form of empowerment for women. I agree. What they will all be able to accomplish after this pageant is staggering. The pageant already aids the Make-A-Wish Foundation, breast cancer research, and AIDS research, and each contestant devotes a serious amount of time to a specific cause. Marco also noted the steady progression of confidence developing in each young woman as the weeks progressed. All in all, a good score.

The ratings for the Miss USA pageant this year were the highest they have been in ten years. The event took place in the glamorous and beautiful city of Los Angeles, and the contestants visited Universal Studios, Santa Monica Pier, the *Queen Mary,* and Hollywood. The show itself was held at the Kodak Theatre, home of the Academy Awards, and was covered by Billy Bush and Nancy O'Dell for *Access Hollywood.* The afterparty and the lines to get in reminded me of Studio 54 in its heyday.

After Miss USA is crowned and the credits have rolled, she flies immediately to her new river-view Trump residence in New York, where she will spend her reign pursuing professional goals and making appearances on behalf of our charitable partners. No other pageant system in the world is set up this way. Every other beauty queen stays home until she's called to make an appearance. When not traveling around the world, our titleholders spend every week volunteering during the day and attending A-list events at night.

As Miss USA 2004, Shandi Finnessey is an official spokesperson for breast and ovarian cancer awareness. She will assist in raising millions of dollars on behalf of these organizations. The benchmark is enormously high, as Miss USA 2003, twenty-four-year-old Susie Castillo, helped raise $28 million for the same cause. Shandi happens to be a gorgeous blonde who is working toward her doctorate in counseling, and she is an advocate for mentally challenged children. Shandi has traveled to Korea with the USO to entertain troops and will travel later in the year to the Middle East.

When a woman becomes Miss Universe, her world is turned upside down. Before Jennifer Hawkins, Miss Universe 2004, left her home in Australia for the pageant in Quito, Ecuador, she was able to be in Sydney without being recognized. Now, having been featured on the cover of every magazine and newspaper Down Under, and having been the subject of several television shows, she has become an instant celebrity. In her new role as a spokesperson for HIV and AIDS awareness, Jennifer has been a moderator at the International AIDS Conference in Bangkok, and she will spend the year meeting world leaders focused on this terrible pandemic. She is also one of the most beautiful women I have ever seen.

Tami Farrell, the nineteen-year-old Miss Teen USA 2004, hails from a farm in Phoenix, Oregon. She has spent the year as an advocate for DARE! and other teen-related causes. Prior to the pageant, she had never left Oregon; now she has traveled all over the United States in addition to a first-class trip to London and Berlin.

When they are not globe-trotting, these three beauties are roommates, which can sometimes be more traumatic than the *Apprentice* apartment. Bill Rancic never had to worry about a misplaced $100,000 tiara.

The Mar-a-Lago Diet

You can't just think like a billionaire; you have to eat like one, too. Whether you have a world-class chef preparing all of your meals a simple hot plate, always remember: You are what you eat.

Gary Gregson, the executive chef of the Mar-a-Lago Club and the Trump International Golf Course, has worked for me for nine years, and he's one of the top chefs in the world. His job is to make sure that all of our guests eat well during their stay. The guests include national and local politicians, television personalities, movie stars, musicians, and the wealthiest of the wealthy. Gary's job is demanding, but he's an absolute pro.

Gary used to keep a list of all the notables who have been entertained at the Mar-a-Lago Club, but the list got too long. There are just too many people who want to experience Mar-a-Lago.

What keeps them coming back? Gary tells me that it's his food, and I'm inclined to believe him.

You may not believe me, but I keep to a somewhat strict diet—a diet that Gary invented for me. We call it the Mar-a-Lago Diet, and if I didn't adhere to it from time to time, my waistline would be an absolute disaster. I'll admit that I go for the occasional DT Burger, or ice cream, or pizza, but for the most part, I watch what I eat.

How do you go about getting started on the Mar-a-Lago Diet? Visiting the Mar-a-Lago Club is a good start, but you can also try it at home.

Gary developed the Mar-a-Lago Diet with me in mind. He tells me that it has a lot in common with some other popular diets out there right now, but the Mar-a-Lago Diet is more sustainable and far more realistic. And it works. A former Miss Universe who had gained some weight stayed at Mar-a-Lago, and after a couple of weeks she was back in pageant shape.

Gary believes it's ridiculous to think you can enjoy life without carbohydrates and sugar. Everyone's avoiding bread, pasta, rice, and potatoes these days. Next month people will probably be swearing off fruits and vegetables. You have to satisfy your appetite and stay balanced. It's as simple as that.

The Mar-a-Lago Diet is not what you can't eat but what you can—and should—eat to stay thin. Part of the Mar-a-Lago Diet is always fulfilling your cravings as they develop, as ridiculous as those cravings may be. Gary's motto may as well be: "Want caviar on your Dover sole? No worries! What about caviar on your scrambled eggs? Even better!"

Breakfast might consist of an egg-white omelet with spinach, tomatoes, and a little feta cheese, a small cup of tropical fruit, and a mimosa made with freshly squeezed orange juice.

Lunch could be a small portion of tilapia and steamed vegetables with fresh herbs and extra virgin olive oil, served with yogurt sauce on the side, iced tea with lemon, and fresh blueberries for dessert.

Dinner depends on whom you are dining with. If you're eating alone or with your spouse, you can cut back a bit. When you're dining with guests and friends, you should indulge a bit more. One of my favorite meals at Mar-a-Lago is lemongrass-infused salmon with scallion pancakes. I also enjoy the yellow-heirloom-tomato gazpacho, with summer squash, and lingonberry sorbet, which is out of this world. I tend to be a little more partial to meals that include Caesar salad, meat loaf, strip steak, or roast chicken, and you should adjust your diet based upon your own tastes.

With immediate family and close friends, there tend to be larger portions and multiple courses. Pan-seared foie gras with spiced pumpkin bread and wild Maine blueberries followed by mango soup with shallot flan is one of Gary's classics. He also serves Parmesan-crusted sea bass with celeriac potatoes, bok choi, and sauce beurre blanc. To finish the meal, even if you're on the Mar-a-Lago Diet, Gary often provides a selection of minuscule desserts or an incredible Grand Marnier soufflé.

If you're a drinker (which I'm not), enjoy a glass of fine wine, but don't overindulge in alcohol. It can be a high-calorie and dangerous habit.

I once asked Gary to tally up the food orders during the busiest part of Mar-a-Lago's season. Apparently, it's not unusual for the club to purchase one hundred pounds of Florida stone crab, forty pounds of fresh grade-A foie gras, twelve points of high-grade caviar (osetra, beluga, or sevruga), and four hundred pounds of sea bass—each week! And, of course, all of these foods work within the Mar-a-Lago Diet.

To summarize the Mar-a-Lago Diet:

1. It has to be served in a fantastic setting.
2. It has to look fantastic.
3. It has to taste incredible.
4. It cannot make you gain weight.

If you eat the best foods and watch your waistline, you'll begin to look and feel great in no time.

Saturday Night Live

One day in late March 2004, Jeff Zucker, the brilliant president of NBC, called to make an appointment to see me at my office. I knew something big must be up for him to pay a personal visit. He said, "I'd like to see you." So he arrived at my office and said, "Donald, do me a favor. Host *Saturday Night Live.*"

I like and respect Jeff a great deal, and we'd been experiencing a tremendous success with *The Apprentice,* so I couldn't say no.

I'd like to say that I showed up a few hours before the show on Saturday, April 3, tried on some costumes, learned a few lines, and then did the show live with the help of the hilarious *Saturday Night Live* regulars. As with *The Apprentice,* that wasn't the case. It took up a few days of my time—a few days well worth it, as experiences go.

Saturday Night Live is a legendary show, and being asked to be the host was a great honor. Considering its twenty-nine-year history, I was walking into something big and something new to me: comedy skits, a monologue, a face-to-face with someone who imitates me for a living, a chicken number. Were they joking? Yes, and quite well.

Here's how the show came together that week:

PREPARATION

On Tuesday, I met with Lorne Michaels's terrific team of seventeen writers, led by Tina Fey. They pitched ideas and asked questions. We chatted for about one hour. How much could they get in one hour? Plenty, as it turned out.

On Wednesday, the writers had various sketches completed, which they presented to me in a series of read-throughs. Some of these writers have been at *SNL* for over a decade, five are new this year, and one was new that week. The job of an *SNL* writer is tough. There's no fooling around. Lorne Michaels and Marci Klein certainly know what they're doing.

After a variety of sketches were finished, they narrowed them down to approximately twelve skits considered viable for the show. This process took about three hours, and then I was free to go back to my office.

On Thursday, we read through the chosen sketches, where I interacted with members of the *SNL* team and got a feel for the format of the show.

On Friday, we had our first full day, which started at 1:30 P.M. and ended at 10:30 P.M. We blocked and did run-throughs of the skits on undressed sets on the *SNL* stage. That space is historic; it was originally Toscanini's recording studio and was built on springs to avoid the rumble of the subways underneath the NBC building. It has about seven thousand square feet of workable space, which isn't a lot, considering what the show accomplishes every week.

In the first skit, I played a hippie in a business meeting about the worldwide marketing of bongs. After three quick run-throughs, I realized that I was dreading having to wear the long blond wig they'd picked out for me. Luckily, this skit would be cut during dress rehearsal. I hate messing up my hair for any reason, even for *SNL*.

On the way to the next skit, I stopped and chatted with Greg

Tull, who has worked at *SNL* as head of props for twenty-five years. He's also a fellow graduate of the New York Military Academy. He reassured me when he told me I was doing a great job so far—a vote of confidence I trusted, as he's watched countless rehearsals over the years.

The second skit involved my so-called latest romance novel, *Erotic Moonlight Confessions*. The protagonist, Ronald Strump, lives in a famous skyscraper in the penthouse apartment with citywide views. Convinced it will be a bestseller, I happen to be the narrator. As it turned out, this favored sketch of mine (short and easy) would also be cut after dress rehearsal.

We took a short break, so I returned to my dressing room, passing the pretzel and potato chip bins, and made a few phone calls and checked in with the office. The very talented Jim Dowd of NBC showed up to give me a tour of the control room. I had gotten to know Jim while working on *The Apprentice*—he doesn't stop. *Saturday Night Live* is a big operation, and everyone involved is a pro.

Back on the set, Stone Phillips of *Dateline* stopped by to visit. He had been down at my Mar-a-Lago Club in Florida over the past weekend doing a story. Then Lorne Michaels came in to say hello. The set was buzzing with activity, and through the windows above the audience bleachers, we could see the NBC tour participants watching us. They waved and gave me the "You're fired!" gesture. Just what I needed: some votes of confidence. Fortunately, they hadn't seen enough yet to pass judgment, so I waved back.

Then I had some rehearsals, one with Finesse Mitchell for a lawyer-client skit that included the Harlem Globetrotters, and another with Darrell Hammond, the brilliant impersonator who can nail just about everyone from Bill Clinton to Regis Philbin to me. The skit was titled "The Prince and the Pauper," and it required a costume change mid-scene that the writers were still trying to nail down.

By then it was 6 P.M. and we were on dinner break. Jeff Richmond came in with a keyboard to go over some lyrics with me for the "Boardroom Band" scene. It only took about five minutes. Andrew, an accommodating page at *SNL*, brought in a steak for me from the Palm. It arrived with plastic utensils. I made a stab at it, but Andrew ran up to Lorne's office to find some silverware for me. I found some golf to watch on TV and relaxed for a while.

A bit later, I signed a dollar bill for the Friday Raffle, an *SNL* tradition. This raffle is a big event, announced by drumrolls on the set, and the crew tried to pull one on me by announcing my name as the winner. However, I already knew the buzz around there. It turned out that Lonnie in wardrobe was the winner.

So it was back to the set for the "Boardroom Band" scene, the most complicated scene for me, as I had to play the keyboard, sing, and remember some complex lines and lyrics. Where was Billy Joel when I needed him?

We did the "Chicken Wings" number (involving Trump's House of Wings), which seemed to be popular right from the start. I kept thinking, "How do I get myself into these things?" I had nixed the chicken outfit, but I did see a strange-looking yellow suit around the set, which had me worried.

We took a break, and Lorne visited me for a while. Carolyn Kepcher arrived to run through her scene. She was relieved to know her lines were limited. Scripts aren't her thing, either.

I went back out to practice the opening monologue. The monologue had to be the most difficult part of the show. I would come out onstage, address millions of people, and hope to be funny. I asked the set builders, "How'd I ever get into this? I should be building, like you. I can relate to you guys." We practiced the monologue a couple of times, with Darrell as my "understudy" and with Jimmy Fallon playing Jeff Zucker. We got some good laughs, and then we called it a night. It was already 11:00 P.M. by then.

THE LIVE SHOW

We had a 1 P.M. call, and I was there on time. Saturday would be another rehearsal on dressed sets and a semi–dress rehearsal. We made changes as we went along, so I had to play close attention all day long.

Not surprisingly, that pastel yellow suit showed up in my dressing room. I tried it on and asked myself a few questions—specifically, "What the hell am I doing here?" Chris Kelly, the stage manager, offered me the neon Chicken Wings sign for my office in Trump Tower as a souvenir. My memories would be vivid enough, but it was thoughtful of him.

We ran through the show, which included three encounters with Star Jones of the TV show *The View.* Star was played by Kenan Thompson. I also visited the set of *Live with Regis and Kelly,* as played by Darrell Hammond and Amy Poehler. I liked all the skits but realized that only certain ones would make the live show.

The *Saturday Night Live* setup is theatrical in concept: If the show works for a live audience of three hundred people, it will work for national TV. The dress rehearsal audience is the focus group for the live show. The skits with the best audience response remain in the live show; the others are cut. The dress rehearsal ran from 8 to 10 P.M., and the live show began at 11:30 P.M. Not until after the dress rehearsal would we know the content or the running order of the live show.

We had a dinner break, and I decided to visit the NBC canteen. What a great setup, with all kinds of entrées and salads and seven or eight desserts and puddings. I got some great chicken and mashed potatoes that I took back to my dressing room. Matthew Calamari came to visit and ended up joining me for dinner. George Ross and Carolyn Kepcher also arrived for dress rehearsal, so they visited for a while, too.

Steve Higgins of the *Saturday Night Live* team came in to go over some writing issues, as skits were still being fine-tuned. I heard the guest band, Toots and the Maytals, practicing out on the set. They sounded terrific, and I went out to listen to them for a while. My daughter Ivanka had told me how great they are, and she was right. The music relaxed me, and surprisingly, I was not at all nervous.

At that point, the fantastic Sharon Sinclair, a makeup artist, took me to get ready for the dress rehearsal, and by 8 P.M. the show had begun before a live audience. I had a few friends and colleagues there, so I knew that I could count on a few free laughs. One half hour of the show would be cut, and I was curious to see what would go and what would stay.

Unfortunately, some of my favorite skits were cut: the Finesse Mitchell tour de force, the audio version of my new romance novel, and a couple of close encounters with Star Jones, but all in all, it would still be a great show.

Melania, Don, Jr., Ivanka, Eric, John Myers, John Mack, and some of my best friends had arrived, and their presence was a big comfort, considering what I was about to do. Then the music started up, and it was showtime—live, this time, in front of the world.

The live show was an hour and a half long, a total whirlwind. We had small portable dressing areas set up on the set for fast changes, and an experienced team of dressers, led by Donna Richards, made sure I was ready for each scene. Did I ever think I'd be the star of a hit television series? No. Did I ever think I'd be the host of *SNL*? Not in a million years.

After the show, I signed some photos for the crew, including one that will hang in the hallowed halls of *Saturday Night Live* for all time. It was a night to remember. Both Lorne Michaels and Jeff Zucker seemed pleased with the show, and I thanked them for a wonderful experience.

We all left for the aftershow party. For the record—and this may *be* a record—I got home at 6 A.M. on Sunday. Just in time to get up and read my newspapers and start a new day . . . and to top it all, the ratings turned out to be great!

A Week in the Life

It's become a tradition for me to include a chapter in my books about a typical week in my life. Readers always tell me they like these sections the best, and I don't want to disappoint anyone. Here's a snapshot of this spring, before the second season of *The Apprentice* took over my life. There are some good examples buried within showing how I think about my time, my business, and the people who surround me.

MONDAY

8:30 A.M. I have a meeting with Matthew Calamari, executive vice president, and Norma Foerderer, vice president, about Trump Ice, my new bottled water, and about the YOU'RE FIRED! T-shirts, which we can't keep in stock due to high demand. As problems go, it's a nice one to have. After seeing the popularity of bottled water, I decided to join the competition with my own. It's certainly an interesting market.

During our meeting, Steve Riggio of Barnes & Noble calls in, so I talk to him for a while. He had ordered a huge quantity of my last book, *How to Get Rich,* and called to say he was glad he did. Steve and Len, his brother, have done a great job with Barnes & Noble.

9:00 A.M.   I do a short video in the conference room for Rich Handler's son, Max. It's for a school project. Afterward, he comes into my office, and we give him a tour. I hope he gets a good report card. He will be a winner.

9:15 A.M.   We have a Trump Tower board meeting in the large conference room. Larry Twill is present, as is Sonja Talesnik from my staff, among others. These meetings are important to me, and I never neglect them. That's Lesson Number One in property management. We cover a lot of territory at these meetings: the operations of the buildings—personnel, security, maintenance, construction—as well as the ongoing sales and leasing status of the units. Eric Sacher, of my accounting department, prepares a financial status report of the building, and we discuss improvements and upgrades, such as renovations of hallways and anything that will provide our tenants with the best surroundings.

10:00 A.M.   I call Paul Spengler, of Pebble Beach, to talk about stone walls. Paul's a great guy and full of good advice.

10:15 A.M.   Rhona comes in to tell me that Chris Matthews is ready for our scheduled interview. We're both on time, and it's done quickly and efficiently. Chris is the kind of guy I like playing hardball with.

10:45 A.M.   We all watch Don, Jr., on CNN/Finance. He mentions how he's the original apprentice, and how his interest in our business and working with me have been a natural progression for him. He comes across as focused and intelligent, which he is, and mentions how much he's enjoyed overseeing the redevelopment of Trump Park Avenue. He's done a great job, I might add. This building is the former Delmonico Hotel, a famed hotel that once hosted Ed Sullivan and the Beatles. It's not only beautiful but historic as well.

11:00 A.M. I make and take calls from Scott Butera, Jon Tutolo of Trump Model Management, and Ashley Cooper of Trump National Golf Club in Bedminster, New Jersey. They have positive updates for me, so it's smooth sailing so far. I also take calls from Tony Veneziano, Ray Royce, Jay Neveloff, and Phil Ruffin. These guys all get to the point quickly. It's a pleasure doing business with them.

11:45 A.M. My development team comes in for a meeting, which includes Charlie Reiss, Don, Jr., Russell Flicker, and Jill Cremer. We spend a few moments congratulating Russell on the birth of his daughter Molly over the weekend. Being a father is a great honor, and I'm happy for him. My team is on target on their projects, and Canouan Island is going to be a piece of paradise in no time. Canouan is off the island of Mustique, and it will be the new definition of the word "elite."

Canouan Island was brought to my attention by this team, and it will not only rival Bali in beauty and amenities, it will be much more accessible. We will have an eighteen-hole championship golf course, designed by Jim Fazio and Trump Island Villas, that will consist of luxury villas and estate properties set on one thousand acres of lush mountainous terrain overlooking the ocean. It will also have a European-style casino, Trump Club Privee. This island will be my first venture in the Caribbean, and we are all excited about it.

12:30 P.M. I take a call from Paula Shugart about the upcoming Miss Universe pageant in Quito, Ecuador. This event will be big, and we're going over all the details. The Miss USA pageant broke records this year, and we expect the Miss Universe contest to do even better. People couldn't believe I actually went into the beauty pageant business to make money, but it turns out I have, and we've had great success with them. Beautiful women can be a great attraction.

I ask Rhona to order some pizza for lunch, and I call Regis Philbin to chat. I also spend some time reviewing some reports on my properties. Since the final episode of the first season of *The Apprentice*, I've actually had time to devote myself fully to my properties. I like being a TV star, but I'm a builder at heart and always will be. I told Katie Couric on a recent appearance on the *Today* show that she wouldn't have to see me again for a few months, after I nearly became a regular on their morning lineup. I began calling the *Today* show the *Yesterday, Today, and Tomorrow* show to my staff.

1:00 P.M. I call Mike van der Goes, director of Trump National Golf Course in Los Angeles, for an update. This course is becoming an unbelievable beauty, thanks to Pete Dye's expertise and Mike's daily care. I visited recently on a trip to Los Angeles and can't wait to play when the course opens.

A friend calls in who had recently visited Paris and went to the Lido. In the show, an airplane arrives as a special effect, and the French people seated at the next table exclaimed, "Regardez! Doe-nald Trump est arrivé!" and then proceeded to discuss *The Apprentice*. Apparently, they receive tapes of the episodes from American friends. Guess I'm world-famous.

I get a call about the *Apprentice* sign that had hung in front of Trump Tower until the final episode. It's no longer there, but it caused some media attention, as the city almost fined me for it. The amount of money and tourism *The Apprentice* has generated for the city of New York doesn't seem to matter to city officials. Should I be surprised?

I call Melania to see what time I need to be ready tonight. We're going to the Costume Ball at the Metropolitan Museum of Art, which is a fabulous event in New York City, especially since I don't have to wear a costume. This reminds me of something, and I call Anna Wintour at *Vogue* magazine. She is fantastic!

1:30 P.M.   I call Carolyn Kepcher for an update on activities at Trump National Golf Club at Briarcliff Manor. It should be a great season. Even with all her *Apprentice*-related duties, she's remained as effective and efficient as ever as an executive vice president. She could be categorized as a wonder woman, considering her executive activities, being a regular on a hit TV series, and being the mother of two children. She handles it all.

I take a call from Paul Davis, CEO at Trump Place. He's another gem. He has an enormous property to watch over, and with his amazing talent, I can be assured it's in good hands. This property is not only a property to me but a community. Visit the pier sometime at twilight, and you will have yourself a New York experience to remember.

I go over the lyric sheets for the Katie Couric benefit aboard the *Queen Mary 2* coming up in New York City. I'll be accompanied by Harry Connick, Jr. Since I've already done some singing on *Saturday Night Live,* this event shouldn't be too hard. It should be a great night. I hope Harry can keep up with me. However, according to this script, he fires me. Life, as we all know, isn't fair.

Jay Bienstock and Kevin Harris of Mark Burnett Productions are back in town. They come in to review assignments for the second season of *The Apprentice*. I can't discuss these with you now, but it looks like we're in for another exciting series. I have a comfortable rapport with all of Mark's people, and it's a productive meeting. We'll be shooting an intro scene at the Statue of Liberty next week, provided we can get clearance in these days of heightened security.

2:30 P.M.   I return several calls that came in during the meeting. We are still debating which ballroom chair design we will use out at Palos Verdes, home of Trump National Golf Club/Los Angeles, and several chairs have been brought in and lined up in my office to view and think about. There's a spectacular ballroom at the clubhouse for formal events. I'll keep the chairs in my office for a few days to see how they "sit" with me. The wrong chairs will ruin the entire room. In fact, I'd better see a few more, and I ask that a total of eight styles be brought in. This ballroom has apparently become the number one choice for weddings, and it is booked far, far in advance.

Norma keeps my calendar straight, which has become an even greater challenge these days than ever before. She comes in to update me about the week's important events, board meetings, and so forth. She also tells me of humorous calls. This morning we had an Al Pacino impersonator call to talk to me, a call that almost got to my office until "Al" asked one of my assistants for her phone number. And we received another check for $250,000 from someone who will pay to work here, a phenomenon that has occurred several times in the past few months. If we thought we received a lot of mail and calls before *The Apprentice*, we were right, we did. But we now have ten times that amount, and we are doing our best to keep up with it. However, if it takes a longer time to hear back from us, you'll know why.

3:00 P.M.   Jason Greenblatt comes in to go over a few things, and Bernie Diamond, general counsel, comes in to discuss licensing issues. My legal team is kept extremely busy, and they are conscientious about keeping me informed. Even George Ross, with his commitment of time to *The Apprentice,* has managed to keep up with all the new developments we've encountered as we deal with territory more familiar to a production company than a property management organization. I think we've all enjoyed the new challenges, and no one here can ever complain of boredom.

Dan Roth of *Fortune* magazine calls in to discuss the positive buzz his cover article about me has generated. The article is titled "The Trophy Life: You Think Donald Trump's Hit Reality Show Is a Circus? Spend a Few Weeks Watching Him Work." People are always surprised at how hard I work, which I have to say surprises me, because I don't consider it work—but rather fun.

3:30 P.M. Jeff Zucker of NBC calls, and we discuss the incredible ratings the final episode of *The Apprentice* generated. Close to forty-one million viewers watched. These were stunning numbers for a new show or an old show, and I'm proud of that. If I'm going to do something, no matter what it is, I want it to be great. There have been nearly one million applications received for the second season of *The Apprentice,* which is close to five times more than for the first season. NBC and I are looking forward to the new season.

A reporter calls in to verify that on *Larry King Live* I offered to pay for Troy's education. Troy was on *The Apprentice* and has a lot of smarts but not much formal education. He is a good example of someone who deserves the best, which includes great schooling. Guys like Troy make America great.

3:45 P.M. The next call is a good one. This contractor is so full of it that I hang up on him. Until he comes to his senses, which I think will take at least a few days, considering what I've just heard, I won't be taking his calls. Instead, I call Ron Baron for some levity.

4:00 P.M. My pilot, Mike Donovan, calls in. The most important thing to consider when you have your own 727 is the right pilot to go with it, and I have been very lucky to have Mike.

What is it about Mondays? Here's another contractor who is totally out of his mind. If today were April Fool's Day, I could manage these idiot calls, but it isn't, and this next call also gets a well-deserved slam into the receiver.

Costas Kondylis, a man with brains and elegance, calls, which is a relief from the last few phone calls. We go over some details and discuss the impending Olympics in Athens. Costas is from Greece and has great insights into Greek culture. One reason I like to read Greek philosophers, as I mentioned in my last book, is because of Costas's influence.

I call Tiffany in California. I saw her recently when I attended the Miss USA pageant at the Kodak Theatre in Hollywood. Rick and Kathy Hilton also attended with us, as did Roberto del Hoyo of the Beverly Hills Hotel.

John Spitalny of Bear Stearns calls. We play golf together and enjoy discussing a lot of different things. John gives finance another dimension entirely when he starts in on something. He's an example of someone who applies comprehensive knowledge to specific scenarios. He's an expert of the highest level. He keeps an open mind to everything, and if you ask him a question, he'll find a way to answer you on the level you can relate to most readily.

I call John Stark, another great guy, and take a call from Joe Cinque of the Five Star Diamond Hospitality Awards. We discuss one of our favorite places, the Beverly Hills Hotel, and what makes it so special, which is basically everything. It's a full and total class act. Joe is adamant in his praise for my Mar-a-Lago Club in Palm Beach, which is fine with me. We discuss the new ballroom at Mar-a-Lago, which is close to being finished.

We also discuss the fact that our receptionist at the Trump Organization, Georgette Malone, has returned today after recovering from a vicious attack by a pit bull. Doctors were able to save her fingers and hands, but it's been a long process. We are all happy to have her back in almost one piece. Allow me a few words of advice: Don't keep pit bulls for pets. After seeing what happened to Georgette, I will never forget it, and neither will any of us here.

I take a few calls regarding different properties, and then talk to Elaine Diratz about events at the Trump World Tower. Since people saw the penthouse on an episode of *The Apprentice,* this building has become a hot property. There's a huge waiting list of people wanting to buy!

Tom Downing, general manager of Trump International Hotel and Tower, calls in. Tom was also featured on *The Apprentice* in the semifinal round of interviews, and he's an important member of our organization. We'll be filming a task assignment for the upcoming season of *The Apprentice* at Jean Georges, the restaurant is located in the hotel. Running a great hotel is demanding, but under Tom's leadership, the hotel has been consistently lauded by critics and guests.

4:30 P.M. Allen Weisselberg, my CFO, comes in for a meeting, and then I show him some carpet swatches and ask his opinion. I like to get as many opinions as I can before making a decision. I also ask him about the chairs I'm considering. Rhona comes in, and I ask her opinion as well. These chairs aren't quite right, and I realize that I'll have to ask to see some more.

5:00 P.M. I review some photographs of developments and read a pile of faxes that have come in. We have several fax machines, and they never stop. Then I review a stack of letters. I like to read the ones from students. Some schools have written about each episode of *The Apprentice* and what they have learned from it.

In one class in Illinois, Troy is the most popular candidate, followed by Kwame, and they think New York City looks like a lot of fun. They have sent in twenty-eight handwritten reviews, and while I may not agree with everything they say, I will say I admire their penmanship. I cannot respond to all of them except to thank them for their time and thoughtful comments.

5:30 P.M. I sign a book for Alex Rodriguez, better known as A-Rod, when he comes to our offices for a visit. I take him around and enjoy seeing the surprised expressions on everyone's faces. We peek into a meeting in the large conference room, and everyone does a double take. He's hard to miss, and it's a great way to end a Monday. I had met A-Rod before, as he is looking at an apartment in Trump Park Avenue. He is a great guy and a great player.

6:00 P.M. Robin tells me that one of the crazy contractors I spoke to earlier has called back yet again. They can all forget about it today. Enough is enough. I take some faxes and documents and head upstairs.

TUESDAY

8:45 A.M. I have a meeting with Steve Kantor of Credit Suisse First Boston and Brian Harris, Peter Smith, and Matthew Kirsch of UBS. I like these guys, and our meetings are never a problem. I've always gotten along with bankers, and I appreciate their perspective. People sometimes ask me about the best way to deal with bankers. I always tell them to give them the respect they deserve. That's the best way.

9:30 A.M. I have a Diet Coke and read an article wherein I am called "the Elvis of Business." I'll take it as a compliment. Rhona comes in to give me my messages, and I ask her to return some calls.

I look over some photos from the final episode of *The Apprentice* and from the party we had here at Trump Tower afterward. It was a media circus, but we all had fun. I never thought it would take one hour to walk a hundred feet, but it did. My beautiful sister Maryanne attended but could take only about fifteen minutes of it before slipping out. I find a great photo of her with Norma. I ask Rhona to send it to her.

10:00 A.M. We watch Mike van der Goes, director of Trump National Golf Course/Los Angeles, being interviewed on Fox TV about his job having been offered as one of two choices for *The Apprentice* finalist. Mike had been advised of this possibility, and I have to say I was relieved when Bill Rancic chose the Chicago tower as his project, since Mike is doing such a great job. He also gave a terrific live interview. Fortunately, Mike has many qualifications, including being an accomplished golfer, so we would have been able to find a suitable position for him within our organization without any problem. Versatility is always a benefit for everyone, but we're glad Mike is where he is.

Helmut Schroeder, who manages some properties for me in New Jersey, comes in for a visit, so we chat for a while, and Robin comes in to advise me that Paula Shugart and our new Miss USA, Shandi Finnessey, of Missouri, are here to see me. I'd picked Shandi as my first

Jay Leno and I have a lot in common—we both love our work and a good laugh.

With Melania and Bob Kraft, owner of the New England Patriots.

With Jeff Zucker, president of the NBC Universal Television Group.
Jeff is a total dynamo.

Melania and me with Baron Hilton, a wonderful guy.

On the Today *show with Bill Rancic, Kwame Jackson, and Lester Holt.*

With Garth Brooks, who writes: "Donald—swing harder!"

Melania and me with baseball great A-Rod.

With race car driver Jeff Gordon.

With Governor Arnold Schwarzenegger—he's doing a great job.

Here I am with the dynamic Katie Couric.

*With Suzanne and Bob Wright. Bob is the chairman and CEO
of NBC Universal, and Suzanne is the best.*

Melania and me with Jonathan Tisch.

With my good friend Regis Philbin.

On the course with Nick Faldo.

With Jean-Georges Vongerichten and Mark Burnett,
at Jean Georges restaurant in Trump International Hotel & Tower.

(left to right) Norma Foerderer, Jeff McConney, Matthew Calamari, Eric Sacher, and Allen Weisselberg visit my dressing room at Saturday Night Live.

*Jay Bienstock and Kevin Harris,
producers for Mark Burnett,
with Rudy Giuliani in
Rudy's new offices.*

*Bill Rancic in the media crush
in Trump Tower after
winning* The Apprentice.

With the remarkable Annika Sorenstam.

With Mark Burnett and another one of his big ideas.

The 2004 Miss USA contestants with me and Jay Leno, after appearing on his show.

Trump Place ribbon-cutting.

The Salute to Israel parade on Fifth Avenue. Dr. Ruth joined me for a block or two.

Carrying the 2004 Olympic Games torch in Manhattan.

choice during the pageant in Los Angeles, and I was right. She's a beauty.

Tom Barrack calls in. Tom is one of the smartest real estate investors in the United States. He is looking to invest in my ninety-story building in Chicago. He heads the Colony Capital Fund, and I built a building at 610 Park Avenue with Tom. It's been a terrific success. Not only is Tom a brilliant investor, he is also a great friend.

10:30 A.M. Our mysterious Al Pacino impersonator calls in again. Whoever he is, he's pretty good, but not good enough. We finally get rid of him. I really doubt that Al Pacino is anxious to apply as a candidate for *The Apprentice*. We call Al's office and let them know someone is impersonating him.

11:00 A.M. Norma comes in to advise me of the funeral service for Estée Lauder, who recently passed on. She was one of the most remarkable people I have ever known, and I am sorry she's gone. She left a beautiful heritage, and she will never be forgotten. Her "little business," as she referred to the cosmetics line she founded, controls forty-five percent of the cosmetics market in U.S. department stores. She had an idea and went with it. She was one of the great salespeople of all time and a great example for all businesspeople.

Steve Florio of Condé Nast calls, and then I watch the cut of the new commercial I filmed last week for Visa. It gets a big laugh from my staff. I hope the TV audience likes it as much as they do. At first I thought it might not be so good for my image to be seen in a Dumpster scrounging around for my credit card, but I like to expand my range whenever possible, and fortunately, this is only a role. I do, however, think Visa is a great card to have, or I wouldn't endorse it, especially at this extreme.

I take a call from Random House about my new book and tell them I've been able to find the time to work on it. I like writing books, and if I like something, I can find the time for it. They seem to take my word for it, considering I've got a good sales record. We had two book signings last week, at Grand Central and at the Borders on Wall Street. The turnout was amazing. I enjoyed meeting the people who showed up.

11:30 A.M.   You'd think it was still Monday, since another contractor just called me. If you think I make up this stuff about them, you're wrong. And I'm not out to get them. It's just that facts are facts, and what they present me is another story entirely. I cool down before I blow up by looking out the window and wondering whether I should call Darrell Hammond of *Saturday Night Live* to fill in for me for a while.

Kevin Harris comes up to take me down to the set for the new season of *The Apprentice*. The boardroom was left intact, but the living quarters have been redone. It looks terrific.

12:00 noon.   I go with Brian Baudreau to a meeting at Trump World Tower at the UN Plaza. We also go to the sales office and meet with Elaine Diratz. I absolutely love this building. Once I walked all the way up—ninety floors—just to get the feel of it when it was completed. That wasn't an unusual occurrence with my buildings—it happens from time to time.

Brian, who has been with me for seventeen years, will be moving to Las Vegas this summer to be the owner's representative for my new tower there. Brian has been with me long enough to have a terrific eye and insights into everything and everyone, and I'm pleased to make him an executive.

1:00 P.M.   Back in the office, I see Robin eating a great-looking chef's salad from the Trump Food Court downstairs and ask her to order one for me. I start returning calls that came in from my daughter Ivanka, Rick Hilton, and others. Next month is an important event: Ivanka will be graduating from Wharton. Someone once commented that while getting into Wharton isn't easy, getting out is even harder. She got great marks, and I am extremely proud of her.

1:30 P.M. I take a call from Bob Wright. We're on for dinner next week with his beautiful wife, Suzanne. I feel lucky to enjoy the people I do business with, and Bob's a perfect example. We discuss Jeff Zucker's comment in *The New York Times:* "It turns out that the next *Friends* was not a half-hour scripted comedy. It was *The Apprentice.*"

I take a call from Mark Burnett to review the possible task assignments that have been developed so far for the new season of *The Apprentice.* I've learned that some ideas sound great but don't translate too well onto the screen. For example, writing a presentation might seem like a good assignment until you realize it's passive, there's not enough action, and it would be boring to film and for the audience to watch. Since we are filming in an exciting place like New York City, locations are also important considerations. The details are myriad concerning this show.

2:00 P.M. Don, Jr., and Andy Weiss come in for a meeting. They make a good team, and they're both great workers. I'm not sure which of the two has the messiest office, though; it could be a tie.

Laura Cordovano calls in from Trump Park Avenue sales. All is going well there, and I decide to call Susan James at the Trump International Hotel and Tower sales office. I like to check up on every property myself. Sounds like smooth sailing all around. Great properties can make life in the real estate industry a lot more fun for everyone involved. Great markets aren't bad, either.

Bernd Lembke of the Mar-a-Lago Club calls to brief me about the ballroom proceedings and other work being done on that property. We discuss the moldings around the mirrors, and I'll check them out for myself next weekend.

2:30 P.M.   Verne Gay, the television critic of *Newsday,* calls. In one of his stories, he said amazingly nice things about me, including the fact that I'm "the greatest star in the history of reality TV."

Boxing promoter Don King calls. Don is a real character whom I have known for a long time. He is a big believer in "the look," and every time he sees me, he starts shouting, with his magnificent voice, "Don, you have the look! You have the look!" Well, I agree that Don also has "the look." The look certainly does mean something!

I speak to Herbert Muschamp of *The New York Times,* who is doing a review of one of my buildings. Herbert has been very nice to me over the years, and I hope he continues to be, but regardless, he is a truly talented architecture critic and a really great guy.

3:00 P.M.   Bill Rancic, winner of the first season of *The Apprentice,* is here to visit. My staff greets him warmly, and he makes the rounds of the office to meet all of his new colleagues. I think he'll fit in nicely, and we're happy to have him aboard. We have a meeting in my office with Charlie Reiss, Russell Flicker, and Don, Jr.; Charlie oversees the Trump Tower Chicago development. Bill is handling everything well and does not seem to be daunted by the heavy pressure to do a good job. I have to say, his focus is impressive, and I hope it stays that way.

3:45 P.M.   I make a call to my good friend John Myers of GE. His son was wounded in Iraq, and I want to know how he is doing.

John Burke and Scott Butera come in for a meeting, and we are interrupted by a fire drill. Since September 11, I find that people no longer complain very much about the once-inconvenient fire drills. They're very important. John is an executive vice president and treasurer, and Scott is the director of corporate finance and strategic development. Scott is a great young talent who will soon be heading the casino company. We discuss casino operations and refinancing, specifically the Credit Suisse First Boston investment in the proposed recapitalization of the casino companies. It is very interesting.

4:30 P.M. Robert Morgenthau, one of the greatest of the greats, calls. His dedicated work for the Police Athletic League has been ongoing for forty years now, and he is one of the most respected prosecutors in the history of the American justice system. We will be honoring him at the annual PAL Superstar Dinner at the Pierre Hotel in June, and I am pleased to be the chairman of this event. We are looking to raise $1.7 million for PAL, a record. Bill Clinton will be the presenter.

Bill Carter of *The New York Times* calls to ask me questions about *The Apprentice*. Bill is a very talented and respected television reporter who was the first to point out that it was not merely the success of *The Apprentice* on Thursday nights that was so impressive, but in particular its tremendous success when it was rerun on Wednesday nights and many times on CNBC. Bill felt that without all of these weekly reruns, the numbers on Thursday nights would have been even better, if that is possible.

Rick Reilly of *Sports Illustrated* calls, but I don't take his call. I've heard some negative reviews of Rick Reilly's reporting, and after reading his chapter on me in his book *Who's Your Caddy?*, I would have to say I agree with the critics. I totally disagreed with many of

Reilly's statements in the chapter on me, and the claim that I go around calling people "baby" is just ridiculous. The rest is too trivial to mention, but even though Rick, for the purpose of his book, was supposed to be my caddy, I talked him into a match with me. Rick is a good golfer, a five handicap, but he had a bad day. We played with no strokes, and at the end of nine holes he was nine down, and at the end of eighteen holes he was fourteen down. Rick told me it was the worst beating he had ever had, and I told him there was no way he would mention this in his book. He said, "No, Donald, I will indeed mention it. I got creamed." I again reiterated that "you will never say how badly you lost." In the end, he made reference to losing but nothing like what really happened that day. Only the caddies and my staff know for sure. Well, at least Rick said that Trump National Golf Club in Westchester is a great course. I have a feeling I won't be playing with Rick again.

During the course of our round, Reilly spent a lot of time talking about *Sports Illustrated*, ESPN, and his new contract. I thought he was playing one against the other. I told him he should stay with *Sports Illustrated* out of loyalty. I said, "Don't be a pig, and stay with the people that got you there—it's a little thing called loyalty." He ended up signing with *Sports Illustrated*.

I decide to take a walk down the hall and visit Jeff McConney and Eric Sacher. On the way, I see George Ross, so we have a short conversation and he tells me that eating lunch downstairs at the Trump Grill can sometimes be a lively event now that people recognize him from the show. George can handle it, and sometimes he even smiles at people.

I receive a copy of an article by writer and editor Patricia Baldwin, who interviewed me for *Private Clubs* magazine. She begins the article with a quote from baseball Hall of Famer Dizzy Dean: "It ain't braggin' if you can back it up." Her conclusion: I'm not a braggart, just incredibly good at my job. Patricia spent a day with me while I visited my golf course in Palos Verdes, California.

5:15 P.M.   I take a look around my office and realize I should try to downsize some of the piles of paper, so Norma comes in and we start sorting and sifting. We end up with shorter piles, but more of them. It's a start. I can actually see people on the other side of my desk now. Norma tells me that since her appearance on the show, people have stopped her on the street and in restaurants, and even on the bus, for an autograph. Our lives have definitely changed.

I get a call from Bob Kraft, who owns the New England Patriots. When Bob bought the Patriots, they were a disaster, and now they're the best team in football and the Super Bowl champions. Bob is an extraordinary man who has done an extraordinary job, and he has the best quarterback in football, Tom Brady, who is also a friend of mine.

I review the faxes of the afternoon, decide whether or not I have time to accept public speaking engagements, and look through photographs for a magazine request. Considering that taping for the new season of *The Apprentice* will start up in less than ten days, we have to be careful about the time I have for activities not directly involved with my business at the Trump Organization. I'm not playing hard to get; I just have to keep my priorities in order. Norma knows how to handle my schedule and decline invitations thoughtfully, and that's one reason why she's a great gatekeeper.

My son Eric calls. He'll be attending Ivanka's graduation next month, along with everyone else in the family.

6:00 P.M. Jay Bienstock and Kevin Harris come by to go over some more ideas for the *Apprentice* tasks. This step is an important part of the show, and I like being actively involved with the decisions. Also, it helps that I am a native New Yorker and know the territory well. We spend an hour or so going over a lot of details and thinking through a few possibilities.

7:00 P.M. George Steinbrenner calls. No matter who I might be with, if they hear George is on the phone they are impressed—he is a true winner, and he is always like a jolt of adrenalin. I love George and his winning way!

I'm ready for a busy night in New York City, so I call it a day and go home.

WEDNESDAY

8:00 A.M. I decided to come down a little early today to catch up on some of my mail. Here's a letter from a high school student in Wichita, Kansas, who writes: "Although your story of business success is inspiring, I have another, more unusual reason for making you my hero: You live richly. Although it may sound strange, I'm tired of the people that truly do something to earn their fortune sitting around on it without using it. Finally, in you we have found a man that lives richly." That's a nice comment though actually, I lead a much more simple life than people would believe—but I don't want to disappoint this young man.

Here's a letter from a guy who remembers my father helping him change a flat tire when he was a young man in Queens. He now makes documentary films and wrote to tell me he will never forget my father's kindness. Neither will I.

8:15 A.M. My first phone call comes in, from Paul Spengler of Pebble Beach. It's 5:15 in the morning in California, and he's already up and at it. My kind of guy!

Norma comes in to tell me of her meeting with Random House about the three-book gift set being planned for the Christmas holidays. We have to think ahead these days.

Richard LeFrak comes in to view the construction on his building from my office, which directly faces it. The curtain wall he is erecting now looks perfect. He's another guy I like doing business with, and our meetings are always lively and fun. Richard mentions that my office seems a little cluttered, so I show him Norma's office and our small conference room, both of which are completely covered with bins of fan mail, proposals, and letters that we haven't been able to get to yet. We've been receiving up to twenty bins of mail a day, and we've had to hire six people just to sort it all. So I start a little earlier each day, as do a lot of us here. In showing Richard our offices and what's been happening here, I notice most people are already here, and our day doesn't officially start until 9 A.M. We're all trying to keep up.

8:45 A.M. I go downstairs with Richard to show him the set and living quarters of *The Apprentice*. The new *Apprentice* candidates are due to arrive in under a week, and it's looking good.

9:15 A.M. The calls have begun, so I begin to return them. Jerry Schraeger, Tom Bennison, Lee Rinker. Lee is the golf pro at Trump International Golf Club in Palm Beach, and I enjoy talking about the game with him. He's explaining how a winner's strategy will include losing, and the greats will have a contingency plan close at hand. There's a reason golf is known as a brain game.

9:45 A.M.   Rhona comes in to remind me that I have a lunch with Steve Florio at the Four Seasons today. Seldom do I go out to lunch, but Steve is a friend and the former president and CEO of Condé Nast publications (and I like the guy a lot). Going to the Four Seasons with Steve is always fun and interesting. We cover a lot of territory when we get together, from cross-promoting to publishing to fragrances. Steve is up on everything and has worked with one of the most interesting and brilliant men in business today, S. I. Newhouse.

Jim Dowd of NBC calls to chat. After the media blitz of the past few weeks, we feel like we are having a mini-vacation from each other. Jim is one of those people who is extremely efficient yet easy to work with. An ideal business associate.

Matthew Calamari and his brother Mike come in for a meeting, and I ask Andy Weiss and Don, Jr., to join us. We are still fine-tuning Trump Park Avenue. Putting up the front entrance canopy is a big deal if you're on Park Avenue, and we are using a steel reinforced structure. A work of beauty deserves our total attention, and this building, which has turned out to be a great success, gets it.

10:30 A.M.   Melania calls to see if we are still on for the Broadway opening of *Bombay Dreams* coming up in a couple of weeks. We are, and we've decided to go to Da Silvano, a great Italian restaurant in the Village, afterward for dinner. We try to plan ahead as much as possible.

Jason Binn, the publisher of *Gotham,* calls, and we discuss what's happening on both coasts. Then I read a thank-you note from Mark Cuban regarding his show *The Benefactor.* This note was published on the Web. He mentions that "our encounters proved to be a reality check for me" because he realized he would never want to be like me. But then, I ask myself, why did he buy an apartment in one of my buildings with my name on it? I think it's strange that he's trying to take me on just to get some publicity for his show, but he's actually a nice guy and I hope his show will be more successful than his basketball team. Besides, he has no chance of beating *The Apprentice*.

Kevin Harris comes in for a meeting about my schedule during the second season of *The Apprentice*. I have another week "off," and then it all begins again. I tell Kevin he's a real pain in the ass but I've gotten used to him. He's also gotten used to me, so I can tell him that. He laughs and leaves.

11:15 A.M. Jeff McConney comes in to go over some license issues, followed by Eric Sacher, who updates me on the financials of Trump Model Management. Then I ask Bernie Diamond to come in to review a list of projects, followed by Nathan Nelson, who gives me the latest on our commercial leasing. These guys stay on top of things and are fast at giving me what I need to know. Allen Weisselberg, chief financial officer, comes in to go over sales and acquisition of properties, and we do a general overview. Allen has been with me for thirty years and knows how to get things done. Then Jason Greenblatt briefs me on *The Apprentice*. Six important meetings in forty-five minutes isn't a record, but it's a good indication of how we operate here.

12:00 noon. I call Mark Burnett and we go over a few things. Just because we had one successful season doesn't mean we can take it easy. We are talking about the dynamics of the boardroom scenes, which were the highlight of our episodes so far. We are wondering whether we should expand them or keep them tight and fast like last season. We decide to see how they play out naturally, and take it from there. It's a realistic approach. Mark is an amazing guy, a good friend, and a true visionary. He said my first book, *The Art of the Deal*, had a great influence on him, and here I am, writing a book sixteen years later and mentioning him—the American Dream!

Anyway, back to our boardroom scenes: Sometimes I schedule an hour for a meeting and find it takes no more than ten minutes. Or just the opposite, it will take two hours instead of one. Some things can't be predicted, and as the show is unscripted, that's part of the excitement. Mark's a busy guy, too, and we connect quickly on every issue. He keeps his momentum going, much like I do, which I think is a common denominator in successful people.

Jeff Zucker calls in and we discuss the ratings. This year, ABC had the Academy Awards, CBS had the Super Bowl, and NBC had *The Apprentice*. It is still hard to believe that *The Apprentice* is one of the most successful shows in television history.

I take a call regarding the announcement of my syndicated radio show on Clear Channel, which is to begin in the fall. I've always enjoyed radio programs and have been almost a regular on Howard Stern's and Don Imus's shows over the years. This will be something new and another challenge. I'm looking forward to it. To find time in my schedule, Clear Channel has agreed to record my programs in my office on a weekly basis. I read so many papers and magazines each week that I will never be at a loss for topics, and I will choose to talk about whatever interests me that week. It will be a form of public speaking without the hassle of travel. The sixty-to-ninety-second daily pieces will soon turn out to be the biggest launch of a new show in the history of radio—which is really cool.

12:30 P.M.   I decide to go over to Trump Place on the Hudson River. New York City can be so spectacular in the spring. I can't think of a more beautiful place than this today. Even the river is sparkling. Paul

Davis escorts me around, and the work is going terrifically. Waiting for twenty years to see something come to fruition definitely adds an aura to a project.

1:45 P.M.   Back in the office, I begin returning calls and ask for lunch from the new Trump Grill, which is fast becoming one of the best and most popular restaurants in New York. Norma comes in to go over some upcoming events and business proposals. One lady has written in to ask that I pay for her breast implants, to go along with my credo to "think big." Just when you think you've heard them all!

2:15 P.M.   I have a meeting with architect Andrew Tesoro and Andy Weiss regarding the new clubhouse I am building at Trump National Golf Club at Briarcliff Manor. We call Carolyn Kepcher to discuss a few things.

2:45 P.M.   Steve Wynn of Las Vegas calls. He'll be in New York next week, and we will catch up. He's been interested in *The Apprentice*, so I tell him a bit about the new season.

Then Regis calls. I will be doing a phone interview on *Live with Regis and Kelly* tomorrow morning about some big news that I have. Right now it's a secret.

I take a call from Tony Senecal, my fantastic butler and historian at Mar-a-Lago. Melania and I will be going down to Florida next weekend.

Billy Bush, from *Access Hollywood*, calls, so I talk to him for a while. We all thought there might be a slight media break after the final episode of *The Apprentice*, but we were wrong. Not that I mind, as I like a lot of the media people we deal with very much—Billy, for example. But their interest in the show still surprises me.

I haven't really adjusted to being a TV star yet. For example, one day when I was going to NBC to rehearse *Saturday Night Live,* I walked into the building with Brian, and there were lines of people behind ropes waiting for the NBC tour. Our page was not there to guide us to the elevators yet, so I was face-to-face with about two hundred people who were surprised to see me just standing there. They stared at me in silence, and then our page arrived to direct us to the correct elevator. The silence continued until I got into the elevator, and as the doors were closing, a lady yelled out, "Hi, Mr. Trump! You're fired!"—and everyone else started to scream wildly. I managed to wave back before the doors shut. A funny moment.

Since *The Apprentice* started airing, I am often greeted with a friendly "You're fired!" by people who see me on the street or in a restaurant. Who would have ever believed that phrase would be a replacement for "Hi, how ya doing?"

3:15 P.M.   Don, Jr., and Charlie Reiss come in for a meeting, during which I take a call from my daughter Ivanka. Someday she'll be in on these meetings, too.

Norma comes in to go over requests for speaking engagements. I'll be doing one for Patti Giles in June but have to keep these at a minimum for a while.

4:00 P.M.   Don Thomas is here for a visit. It's always nice to see him. Then I sit in on a meeting in the large conference room with Jill Cremer, Russell Flicker, Don, Jr., and Charlie Reiss. My boardroom is really beautiful. It's an elegant room with perfect lighting. I think people function and think clearly just as well in a well-appointed room as in an overlit and badly decorated one. Businesspeople should think about interiors when they design their offices. Some that I've visited were so dreadful that the only thing I could think of was how to get out of them as soon as possible, and I can imagine their employees may have felt the same way.

4:30 P.M. I call Melania, and we confirm dinner plans with Regis and Joy at Jean Georges for tonight.

Rhona comes in with some faxes, and I begin to return calls that came in during the meeting. One of the contractors has called back several times, but I just won't deal with him yet. There's a difference between "can't deal with" and "won't deal with." Contractors definitely get the latter until they shape up. As for the good ones, I adore them and treat them the best.

5:15 P.M. I review documents and reports and ask that my calls be held, except for urgent ones. George Ross comes in, and we review a few things together.

6:00 P.M. I ask Robin for my calls and return them, and take a call from Kevin Cook of *Golf Magazine*. We'll be playing a round of golf together next month at Trump National/Briarcliff Manor, a course that *Golf Magazine* really likes.

6:30 P.M. I say good night to Norma and Robin and notice that seven or eight more bins of mail have arrived from the afternoon sorting. We'll have to figure this out. Tomorrow.

THURSDAY

8:30 A.M. I have a meeting with Bernie Diamond, general counsel, regarding Trump: The Game, being developed with Big Monster Toys and Hasbro. We have a productive meeting for about half an hour, and then I return a call to Jean-Pierre Trebot, the executive director of the

New York Friars Club. I'll be the guest of honor for their celebrity roast in October, and we discuss a few matters.

9:00 A.M. I have a phone interview with Regis, announcing my engagement to my girlfriend of five years, Melania Knauss. We are both extremely happy being together, and I am fortunate to have her in my life.

9:30 A.M. I do a video in the small conference room for my casino in Indiana.

I return calls to Bob Dowling, Sandy Morehouse, and Vinnie Stellio, who is in charge of many of my projects and is doing a great job. I also talk to Richard LeFrak. Richard has the kind of eye that notices everything.

Some people come in to discuss the leather-bound editions of my books, which are in the works now. I also go over my travel plans for the next few weeks, which have to be worked out around my schedule for *The Apprentice*.

I take a call about my new hotel/condominium tower going up in Chicago. Considering that it is scheduled to open in 2007 and it's sixty percent sold already, I'd say we've received a warm welcome from the Windy City. Chicago's a great place.

10:30 A.M. I take a call from Alfons Schmitt of Palm Beach, and then Chris Devine, chef at Trump Tower Grill and Trump Tower Food Court, comes in for a meeting. I will tell you one of the best-kept secrets in New York City: His DT Burger is the best hamburger in town. It has portobello mushrooms, grilled onions, and Swiss cheese. Try one at the

Trump Tower Grill, and you'll agree. Everything else is great, too, but the burger is my favorite item. I'll be having one for lunch tomorrow. The atrium with the waterfall is also a terrific backdrop for a midtown meal. Check it out once, and you'll be back for more.

Mohamed Al Fayed calls in, so I take his call. It's a pleasure to talk to him. He's calling to congratulate me and Melania on our engagement. Stewart Rahr calls in to tell me he's having lunch delivered for my entire staff today as an engagement celebration because now they'll have an even happier boss. He's right.

11:00 A.M. I leave to go up to Trump National Golf Club in Briarcliff Manor to check out the course and clubhouse. We are ready for the new season, so I want to make a property check myself. Carolyn Kepcher and Vinnie Stellio will meet us. It's another wonderful spring day, and these kinds of trips are one of the many pleasurable aspects of my job.

11:45 A.M. Why not? I'll play a round of golf with John Spitalny and in doing so, do a thorough property check. This course is a beauty all the way. My game is getting there, too. I take it as seriously as I can, considering my schedule. I notice a few things on the property that need to be improved. Notes are taken, and I'm sure things will be taken care of promptly. This is a good operation. I have a chat with Cary Stephan, our golf pro, and then it's time to go.

4:00 P.M. I'm back in the office at Trump Tower, where I return some calls. I speak to the very talented Richard Johnson of the *New York Post* and Shawn McCabe, a young man who has been with me for a long time and is doing a superb job of maintaining and building additions to Mar-a-Lago.

5:00 P.M.   Kevin Harris shows up with yet another monster schedule for me to review. I try to keep the "don't kill the messenger" proverb in my mind as I go over it with him. This guy doesn't stop. He must've been trained by Mark Burnett. Good thing I'm such an easygoing guy.

Someone tells me David Letterman said on his show, "Donald Trump is the biggest star in America, and he won't do my show, but I like him anyway." David's a good guy, always has been, always will be. He's just on the wrong network, that's all. But I'm going to do his show anyway.

I call Melania to see what we're doing this evening, and it looks like it will be Le Cirque. I call in Charlie Reiss to go over some development ideas. Charlie can be blunt—just ask Amy of *The Apprentice*—so we get along just fine. He never wastes my time. I appreciate Charlie's ability to quickly size things up and deliver the goods.

7:00 P.M.   I check in with Matt Calamari and some others, who are still working, and go upstairs.

FRIDAY

8:15 A.M.   Norma and I have a meeting about how to handle the huge amounts of mail we have been receiving. Now I know how publishers or movie companies must feel about submissions, and why they have rules about it. We can hardly walk through our offices anymore, and she shows me where an extra ten or twelve bins have been stored.

8:45 A.M.   I take a call from Bernd Lembke about being in Palm Beach for Mother's Day. That marks the end of the season there for us, and it's always a big day. I'm not big on melancholy, but it's a day for fond memories of my mother, and it deserves a celebration.

I call my sister Maryanne to see if her offer for a home-cooked meal tonight is still on. It is. Not only is she smart, she is a great cook.

9:00 A.M. I have a meeting with Tom Kaufman, Allen Weisselberg, and George Ross; we cover a lot of territory in under thirty minutes.

9:30 A.M. I speak to Bill Fioravanti, who is Paul Anka's tailor. Paul has offered to have a tailored suit made for me—a nice gesture from a nice guy. The suit is great!

I talk to Paula Shugart and Tony Santomauro about the upcoming Miss Universe pageant in Ecuador. The buzz is huge there. I'll be flying down for the event, in between my *Apprentice* assignments.

Speaking of which, here are Jay Bienstock and Kevin Harris at my door. Why did Mark have to hire such efficient guys? At least they know how to give efficient meetings, and we're through in fifteen minutes.

10:00 A.M. I call Sean Compton, vice president and national program coordinator for Clear Channel, regarding my radio program, and Rhona comes in to advise me of an upcoming photo shoot with Scott Duncan. Not my favorite thing, but I like Scott a lot, so it shouldn't be too painful.

I read a few letters. There's one from a young lady in Arizona, who writes: "Finally! A reality show that is as captivating as it is compelling. Maybe it's because I have a degree in business and a law degree . . . or maybe it's because of your no-nonsense approach to dealing with people. Thank you for allowing the viewing public to be a part of this experience." I'm glad to know people are enjoying the show as much as I am.

I make a call to Paul Chapman and ask for a Diet Pepsi. Norma comes in to remind me of the Damon Runyon Cancer Breakfast at the Rainbow Room later this month, honoring the great Bob Wright of NBC, and a few other engagements.

10:30 A.M.   I have a meeting with Bernie Diamond, general counsel, and then Costas Kondylis arrives for a meeting. I ask Don, Jr., to come in, and we have a discussion about contractors, so I call one, and sure enough, he's at least $100,000 over the amount that is necessary to do the job. After I finish talking to him, he's down to a reasonable price, $100,000 less than he had originally figured. Need I say more?

10:45 A.M.   I take a call from John Stark of Stark Carpet and talk to Bernd Lembke regarding the weekend at the Mar-a-Lago Club. I'm happy to report that work on this incredible place will never end. I am now building what will soon become the finest ballroom facility in the United States. I call Tony Senecal to go over a few things.

I take a call from David Hochman of *Playboy* about an interview in May, and have a meeting in the large conference room with my development team to go over plans and to see what's in the works. Part of being a good builder is planning into the future, which is one reason I enjoy these meetings so much. A room with blueprints equals a room with a lot of action in the works.

11:45 A.M.   I go down with a group of Wall Street bankers to show them the new suite for the eighteen new *Apprentice* applicants. They agree that it looks great, and I realize I'm looking forward to having another group of enthusiastic young people to work with. The boardroom looks ready for another dynamic season. We go down to the atrium level. A few people wave and say, "You're fired!"

I take a tour through the beautiful new space occupied by Asprey, the famed jewelers, which covers three floors in the front of Trump Tower. When you see the British flag flying next to the American flag on Fifty-sixth and Fifth Avenue, it's because of Asprey. They are the jewelers to the royal family and many other people of discerning taste.

As I pass through reception back to my office, I stop to ask Georgette how she's doing in her first week back at work. Very well. She's a trouper.

12:15 P.M.   I return the calls that have come in and call Tiffany in California for an update. George Ross comes in for a meeting, and we discuss a few things pertinent to the new season of *The Apprentice*, as well as business issues. Andy Weiss, Bernie Diamond, and Allen Weis-selberg also come in for meetings.

I take a call from Rudy Giuliani regarding a dinner together, and I talk to Random House about a sales conference where I will appear. I told Random House that I wanted to give readers everything needed to be successful in life in fewer than three hundred pages. That's a challenge, and I like to challenge myself as much as possible. But my books aren't strictly educational; they might become less interesting if they were one-dimensional.

Robin comes in to remind me of the Police Athletic League Board of Directors meeting next week, and we discuss some invitations and business proposals that have come up. Here's someone who wants to build a tower on top of Trump Tower with me, after hearing the idea on *Saturday Night Live*. I seriously doubt if this guy knows that *SNL* is a comedy show, and he's decided he's my new partner because he also likes chicken wings. We couldn't make these things up if we tried. In fact, if the *Saturday Night Live* writing team ever runs out of ideas, they should come over here for a day or so and read my mail.

1:00 P.M. I take a call from Wagner College in Staten Island. I will be receiving an honorary doctorate degree in May—certainly an honor. "Dr. Trump" sounds good to me.

It's surprising what a few days of honest reflection and number crunching can do, because one of the contractors from earlier this week calls back and finds he can do the job "easily" for $150,000 less than he'd originally thought. I figured as much, and that's why I finally took the call.

I take a call from Vinnie Stellio, who is checking out the golf course development and construction at Trump National/Los Angeles. We are building a truly great course there.

I make a call to my brother Robert to see what's up. He'll be going to London next week.

I tell Bobby "Hollywood," one of my bodyguards, that I want to take a walk over to Trump Park Avenue. These days that can be quite an adventure, but he's up to it.

1:45 P.M. I arrive at Trump Park Avenue. The lobby looks great, but I want the doormen to be wearing white gloves. After all, this is Park Avenue. I notice some of the woodwork is off-kilter in one of the elevators; I ask that it be fixed immediately and that they take the elevator out of service until it is. I have an eye for little things, which can either amaze people or irritate them, depending on the circumstances. I do a property check, and it's looking good overall, although not perfect, so we go over a few things that need attention. I always pretend that I'm a tenant in all of my buildings. What things would bother me if I were? First of all, everything has to shine, otherwise it just looks lousy. The lobby and the halls have to be in mint condition at all times, all the fixtures should be polished and lit, and the carpeting has to look brand-new, always. Run-down anything looks run-down, and run-down is not acceptable—ever! Most landlords wouldn't want a tenant like me, but that's why most tenants want a landlord like me: Being a perfectionist works to their benefit.

3:00 P.M. Robin has my messages waiting, so I return ten or twelve calls that have come in and review notes from a meeting regarding 40 Wall Street, my jewel of a building in the Financial District. Downtown has made a good rebound. As I told the *New York Post:* "Even 9/11 couldn't put a permanent dent in that place."

Carolyn Kepcher calls in. We go over some notes I made yesterday about Trump National/Briarcliff during my round of golf and afternoon on the grounds. Once the season at Palm Beach winds down, I'm on the course a lot in Westchester, and we are constantly fine-tuning everything.

3:30 P.M. I have a meeting with Charlie Reiss and Bill Rancic concerning the Chicago tower. We go over some brochures for the building. We discuss the Las Vegas tower being planned. I will be building a luxury condominium/mixed-use tower there with Phil Ruffin, one of the greatest guys I know, so I'll be flying out there for a quick visit within the next couple of weeks. You can see why having a jet is a necessity in my life.

I call Katie Couric to congratulate her on the great job she did for the colon cancer benefit on the *Queen Mary 2*. She raised $5 million for this important cause, and she's a great lady, even if she did have Harry Connick, Jr., "fire" me after my duet with him. I'll try to forgive her, but only because I like her so much.

4:00 P.M.   Norma comes in with a stack of letters and proposals to go over. She says I cringe when I see her come in. She's become "the homework queen" in my eyes, and she knows it.

Random House calls to tell me they've sold the rights to *How to Get Rich* to publishers in twenty-one foreign countries. A friend of mine told me his son of sixteen read it three times and wants to run his own organization as a result. Now he even reads financial magazines and papers every day, his favorite being *The Wall Street Journal*. I liked what I was hearing.

I call my son Eric to see what he's got planned for the weekend. He says "studying," but somehow I think otherwise. Not that he isn't a good student (he definitely is), but he's an outdoor type and has a lot of activities that interest him. All of my children are very well balanced as far as being hard workers, and they are disciplined people, so I never have to worry about them too much.

4:45 P.M.   Rhona comes in to give me my latest faxes and messages. I call Steve Wynn and tell him I'll be visiting soon, and I call John Myers, then Mark Brown. Mike van der Goes calls in from California, and Paula Shugart calls in about an interview for a magazine in Ecuador. And of course, another one of those contractors from earlier in the week calls in, with radically altered prices for his services. Why are certain things so predictable? Anyway, it's nice when they become so agreeable—another word for "reasonable" in this case.

5:30 P.M.   I sign a few books to be sent out to friends and colleagues, make a few final calls, and Allen Weisselberg stops by for a few minutes on his way out. It's been a good week, in fact a milestone week for me, and we're all looking forward to the weekend.

6:30 P.M. I turn out my lights and head upstairs. I'm looking forward to some golf this weekend, as we'll be staying in town. We need a weekend just to relax, which means we may visit Atlantic City tomorrow night by helicopter, check out the course in Bedminster, New Jersey, on Sunday, and have dinner at the '21' Club tonight. This weekend will be relatively quiet for us. Trump Tower is a great home base.

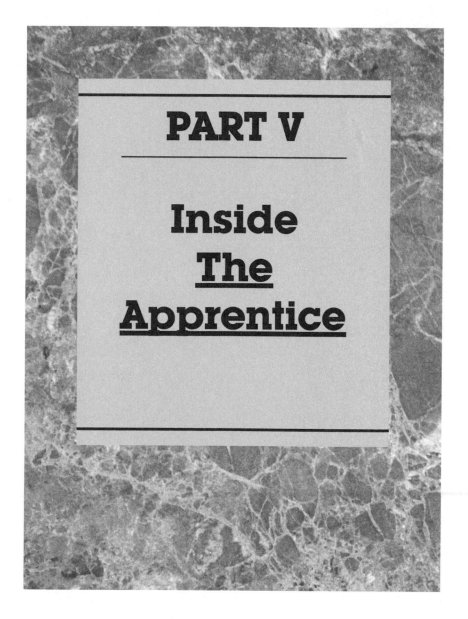

PART V

Inside
The
Apprentice

The Final Episode of <u>The Apprentice</u>

The final episode of the first *Apprentice* series, filmed live at NBC in the *Saturday Night Live* studios, felt for me like a bit of a homecoming. I'd spent a few days there just a couple of weeks before. I knew where the canteen was, I knew where the pretzels were, I knew the wardrobe people, and I knew my way around the set.

Jeff Zucker, Bob and Suzanne Wright, and Darrell Hammond came to visit me, and we even had the same stage managers, Gena and Chris, so it seemed like the continuation of a terrific event. I also noticed that my photograph had joined the *SNL* greats on the hall-of-fame photo gallery that lines the walls as you walk to the set. I was ready for another new adventure.

At 3 P.M. I had an interview with Pat O'Brien, then of *Access Hollywood*, followed by a conference with Mark Burnett to go over the live broadcast. Then we had a lighting rehearsal on the set, where they had constructed a boardroom to emulate the one in Trump Tower. Carolyn Kepcher and George Ross joined me.

I had my old dressing room from *Saturday Night Live*, and the sixteen original *Apprentice* candidates had their dressing rooms one floor up. There was definitely a celebratory feel to the backstage area, a reunion for everyone of a truly great success.

I wondered what property the winner would pick. After all, it's my business, literally, so I was trying to assess the outcome of both possibilities. I had a terrific guy running Trump National Golf Club at Palos Verdes, Mike van der Goes, and I didn't want to lose him or put him into a different position. The tower in Chicago was more open to someone new coming in, because it is still in development, so I was hoping the winner might pick Chicago. But I had two sincere offers out to the winner, and it would be his choice. I'd have to deal with whatever he dealt me.

After the lighting rehearsal, I had another meeting in my dressing room with Mark Burnett and his producers, Jay Bienstock and Kevin Harris. We reviewed the impact of the show and how certain members had been perceived. Two of the contestants in particular had received a lot of attention: Omarosa seemed to emerge as the villain, while Troy emerged as the hero. Recently, someone asked me if I'd give Omarosa a job reference. My answer: I'd give her a good reference for a soap opera.

We also discussed how the group might interact during the live show and whether we might encounter any difficulties. We tried not to leave ourselves too open to any possible blowups or problems, but a live show is always a bit of a gamble. I sent signed copies of my book *How to Get Rich* up to the sixteen while they waited for the show to begin. George Steinbrenner called in to wish me well and said his entire family would be watching. George was behind the show before anyone else.

I went back to visit the friendly and helpful wardrobe team, where I spoke to Dale Richards, who has been with wardrobe at *Saturday Night Live* for eighteen years. He told me there was a buzz in the air, even a bit of nervousness among the *SNL* veterans, because whereas *SNL* has been operating for twenty-nine years, *The Apprentice* was only a few months old at that point. It was new territory for them. They couldn't just relax and expect things to go as usual, because this show was *not* usual. But he said considering my performance on live TV already, they were not concerned about me. They knew I could handle it, and I felt very confident.

What's great about NBC is that they do things professionally and with pizzazz as well. It wasn't necessary, but they had a live band for the final episode, with members of the *SNL* band, which added to the excitement. Just to hear them warming up gave the place the air of a great event about to happen.

As it turned out, it was. Mark Burnett, Melania, and I watched the taped portion of the final episode in my dressing room, and then I went out for the final boardroom scene with Carolyn and George, and Kwame and Bill. We also had the other fourteen candidates on the set, and we gave updates on several of them to the television audience.

It probably helped that I didn't know how huge the TV audience was during those final minutes, but I pretended this show was just another deal for me, so I wasn't too nervous. In a way, it was business as usual, and my choice of Bill to be my apprentice felt right to me. I've never been a histrionic person, so even with an audience watching, I knew what would be the best decision for the Trump Organization. Experience just kicked in and took over.

But I will admit that it was exciting. The culmination of all those weeks of ups and downs—the many assignments, personal problems, infighting, the deviousness as well as the camaraderie—happened incredibly quickly. And, lucky for me, Bill chose the Chicago Trump Tower for his assignment. It seemed to be over so suddenly.

Or so I thought. We had an aftershow party at Trump Tower for everyone involved with the program, and I have never experienced that amount of media in my life. It was a media extravaganza. Fifth Avenue was blockaded, and there were thousands of people there just to see who went in. It took Melania and me over an hour to walk the red carpet from the front door to the elevators, probably a distance less than one hundred feet. It was a crush from every side, but the mood was jubilant, and I can't complain. It was terrific.

NBC, Mark Burnett, and everyone else involved with *The Apprentice* worked so hard, and I had a great experience—one I will never forget. I'm looking forward to the new season.

The Apprentice II

With the worldwide excitement surrounding the first season, the incredible ratings success, and four Emmy nominations, Mark Burnett, NBC, and I knew that we would have to deliver an even better show for the second season of *The Apprentice*. It's going to be incredible, and here is a blow-by-blow of the making of the first four episodes.

MONDAY, MAY 10

Monday, May 10, marked the opening day of filming the new season. Mark Burnett and his team came to my offices to show me the tape to introduce me to the eighteen new apprentice candidates. I would soon be face-to-face with these men and women in the boardroom downstairs.

They looked like a dynamic and energetic group. Type A personalities all the way. Not only do they look good, but their backgrounds include West Point, Princeton, Harvard, and Wharton. Not bad.

At 11 A.M. we all went to the fourth-floor suite, which had been beautifully redesigned by Kelly Van Patter. She did the first season's suite, too, and this one was even better. Jim Dowd of NBC met us there, along with Craig Plestis, senior vice president of alternative programs and development at NBC, and Lee Strauss, vice president of business affairs at NBC, also known as the reality-show "deal maker." I got quite a welcome, and it made me think that maybe I matter to this network, which is a great feeling. As business partners go, NBC is the best.

Carolyn Kepcher, George Ross, and Robin Himmler from my staff were there and ready to go into our second season as regulars, as is Scott Duncan, a photographer with great-looking dreadlocks and talent to match, who is also the brother of Tim Duncan, of the San Antonio Spurs. Mark introduced me to his beautiful girlfriend, the television star Roma Downey, and we gave her a tour of the infamous boardroom. Then it was time to meet the eighteen new candidates in person.

Sitting before the new contestants, I noticed that George was looking especially dapper. I think TV stardom agrees with him. However, I clued in the new eighteen that while both George and Carolyn can be tough and nasty, to watch out—George actually *is* nasty. They laughed. I don't think they believed me.

All of the candidates introduced themselves. They were obviously and understandably nervous, but I could tell that the anticipation level was completely positive. That energy gave me a great first impression of them, and I told them that taking a shot at this show deserves some self-congratulation. They have drive.

I also mentioned that Bill Rancic is doing very well as the winner of the first season, but all the other candidates from that show are certainly on their way as well. There were no losers in this new lineup before me.

Carolyn mentioned to them that only eighteen out of one million applicants were chosen. That should give them a lot of confidence going into the challenges that await them. George, trying to be polite for a change, told them that they were all highly qualified and that he expected them to do a good job.

I also told the men and women that they would be divided into two groups according to gender. I took a lot of heat for that the last time, but that's too bad. I'm not running for office, and it's my decision. They would soon be put through the wringer, and they would feel every emotion—both positive and negative—in the process. But someone would emerge as my apprentice, with another terrific opportunity waiting for him or her at the finish line. It might be a nasty race, but it will also be fun.

With that, they were off to the suite, which had been furnished with plenty of champagne, caviar, and other indicators of their good fortune just to be here today. I think they all felt that way, just as we did.

I found myself wondering whether we had another Sam Solovey in this group. Sam is odd but talented. Some of his quirky behavior didn't make it to the television show. For example, he actually dressed up in an evening gown (not really a pretty sight) for a commercial promoting my Miss USA pageant. Not many people would have done that; I have to give him credit. And the $250,000 that Sam supposedly gave me? It wasn't $250,000 at all, but about $1,100 with lots of newspapers tucked under it. But that's Sam—he's tricky, he's smart, and he'll be just fine.

I had the advantage of introductions to the eighteen new candidates, so here's a brief bio of each of them for you.

Kevin *(Chicago, Illinois), law student*
Kevin, 29, grew up in Silver Spring, Maryland, and then went on to attend the Wharton School of Business. He gave up his pursuit of a professional football career when his brother was diagnosed with leukemia. He later received an M.B.A. in M&A and finance from Emory. He is currently working toward earning his law degree at the University of Chicago. He and his brother have founded their own software company.

Raj *(Vail, Colorado/Philadelphia, Pennsylvania), real estate developer*
Raj, 28, received his secondary education at the Hill School, a boarding school outside Philadelphia, and later earned degrees in both economics and history from Boston College. Moving on from a successful stint in investment banking at the firm of Violy & Co. in New York City, Raj founded Automovia Technology Partners at the age of 23. The company worked closely with some of the largest and most respected firms in the automotive industry to develop custom-built cutting-edge technology related to the valuation and distribution of pre-owned automobiles. After this time in the technology sector, Raj turned his focus to real estate and created Vanquish Enterprises. This led to the acquisition of a hotel, retail, and condominium project in Vail, Colorado. Through an extensive renovation and repositioning of this asset, the project is on track to increase revenue by 300 percent.

Maria *(Virginia Beach, Virginia), marketing executive*
Maria, 31, grew up in Tallahassee, Florida. Her primary residence is in Virginia Beach, where her husband is an FA-18 pilot in the United States Navy. Maria has a B.S. in business and completed her M.B.A. with a specialty track in entrepreneurial marketing. In 2002, Maria was named the youngest vice president in the history of her publicly traded company. She is currently the vice president of marketing for a real estate investment trust company headquartered in Richmond, Virginia, and has ten years of experience in the fields of marketing/branding, sales, business management, and advertising.

Bradford *(Fort Lauderdale, Florida), attorney*
Bradford, 32, hails from a small town in Massachusetts. He later settled in South Florida, where he obtained his J.D. from Nova Southeastern Law School. In addition to being a successful lawyer and handling several high-profile cases, he is also a real estate investor and owns several pieces of commercial and residential property in south

Florida. He can be seen daily, commuting to the courthouse or inspecting his properties in his customized gas-powered golf cart, complete with monster-truck tires.

Jennifer C. *(New York, New York), real estate agent*
Jennifer, 31, graduated with honors and a B.F.A. degree from Syracuse University, and immediately went on to become one of the youngest photo editors hired at a leading international entertainment magazine. Jennifer quickly rose through the ranks, working at many of the country's top-selling publications, producing shoots for some of the world's most famous celebrities. Jennifer soon made a lucrative career change into real estate and was offered a desk at one of the most prestigious firms in New York City, Prudential Douglas Elliman. Though told by her managers that it could take well over six months to close a deal and earn an income, Jennifer went into multiple contracts within her first six weeks in business, impressing even the most seasoned veterans. Jennifer is now successfully selling multimillion-dollar, high-end residential real estate. As her competitive career mirrors, Jennifer also excels as an accomplished award-winning equestrian.

Pamela *(San Francisco, California), investment firm partner*
Pamela, 32, is an accomplished and well-trained business executive who has founded two successful companies from the ground up. She holds an undergraduate degree in economics from the University of Pennsylvania and an M.B.A. from Harvard Business School. During the 1990s, she worked as an investment banker on Wall Street, underwriting IPOs and doing M&A advisory work for two top-tier investment banks. In 2000, Pamela founded Blazent, Inc., from her loft in San Francisco. Blazent has grown to become a successful enterprise-software company, now with offices all across the country. After two years as the company's CEO, Pamela left Blazent to form Crimson Holdings, a private investment firm focused on real estate investments

and equity hedge strategies. The Crimson Funds, including Crimson Advisors and Crimson BridgePoint Funds, have performed exceptionally well, and the Crimson family of funds is quickly becoming a leader in the management of alternative investments.

Sandy *(Rockville, Maryland), bridal shop owner*
Sandy, 28, was born and raised in a Portuguese home in the Washington, D.C., area. By the age of 21, she was the youngest bridal-store owner in the country. Since then, Sandy has evolved to become an exclusive wedding and event planner in the metropolitan D.C. area. Her clientele has included heirs to the Tiffany & Co. family and elite politicians. Sandy's entrepreneurial enthusiasm has also led her into real estate ventures and investments. Presently, Sandy keeps busy growing her award-winning bridal business and wedding-and-event-planning company.

Rob *(Frisco, Texas), corporate branding salesman*
Rob, 32, grew up in Plano, Texas, and later earned a football scholarship to Northeast Missouri State University, where he started four years in the linebacker position. After graduating with a bachelor of science degree from the University of Texas, he and his wife founded Flanagan Enterprises, Inc., and grew it into a multimillion-dollar business, selling corporate-branded items and custom solution-packaging products worldwide. In November 2003 Rob partnered with HotLink, Inc., an industry leader utilizing marketing automation, based in Austin, Texas, where he is VP of Dallas Sales. Along with raising his two young children, Rob enjoys golf, scuba diving, playing his guitar, and fishing.

Elizabeth *(Marina Del Ray, California), marketing consultant*
Elizabeth, 31, has more than thirty Fortune 500 companies and over forty multimillion-dollar brands relying on her to help them develop

creative ideas to build their businesses. Elizabeth currently owns and runs Pulse40, a successful consulting firm, where she pioneered a unique interviewing process. With products ranging from laundry detergent to movies, you might recognize much of her work on TV today. Elizabeth graduated with a 4.0 from the University of Michigan Business School, where she was recognized as an Angell Scholar, received the Branstrom Prize, and was ranked in the top one percent of the nation for academic excellence and leadership. Elizabeth's professional foundation began when she was hired by Procter & Gamble Brand Management and very quickly became a highly successful brand manager. Fun facts most people don't know about Elizabeth are: she's a published poet, state champion basketball player, avid Salsa dancer, motivational speaker, and an award-winning short-film director.

Stacie J. *(New York, New York), sandwich shop owner*
Stacie, 29, grew up in Colorado. She has a B.A. from Emory University and an M.B.A. from Mercer University, both of which are located in Atlanta, Georgia. She is a professional model with Ford Model Management, based in New York City, and Elite Model Management, with offices in Los Angeles, Atlanta, Miami, and Chicago. She currently owns a successful Subway sandwich shop franchise in Harlem, New York.

Andy *(Boca Raton, Florida), recent Harvard graduate*
Andy, 23, was born and raised in south Florida, where he recognized early on what it would take to succeed in business. At the age of 13, Andy co-founded a concert package company that focused on both corporate and individual clients. As the youngest of four boys, Andy learned to use his speaking skills to defend himself at an early age. In 1999, he utilized those verbal skills to win the U.S. National Debate Championship in Commentary Speaking. Andy is a recent graduate of Harvard University, where he was a founding member of an organiza-

tion dedicated to fighting infectious diseases in developing countries. A competitive tennis player, Andy is looking forward to continued success both in and out of the Boardroom.

Ivana *(Boston, Massachusetts), venture capitalist*
Ivana, 28, earned her B.S. from the McIntire School of Commerce at the University of Virginia, with a concentration in finance. She has spent the past five years in the venture-capital industry, investing in technology companies. Ivana enjoys running and cycling, and recently raised five thousand dollars for the Leukemia and Lymphoma Society by completing a one-hundred-mile ride around Lake Tahoe. She lives in Boston with her fiancé, Brian, who attends Harvard Business School.

Jennifer M. *(San Francisco, California), attorney*
Jennifer, 29, received her undergraduate degree in English from Princeton and her law degree from Harvard. She graduated magna cum laude and Phi Beta Kappa from Princeton, and was nominated for the Pyne Prize, Princeton's highest honor. She is currently a securities litigator for a law firm in San Francisco and has worked with management teams from start-ups to Fortune 500 companies. Jennifer lives in San Francisco with her husband, Aron.

Wes *(Atlanta, Georgia), private wealth manager*
Wes, 27, grew up the son of a veterinarian and the eldest of four rambunctious siblings, learning responsibility and leadership at a very young age. Wes hails from Atlanta, Georgia, where he lives with his wife, Lynne. He holds an economics degree from the University of North Carolina at Chapel Hill. Postgraduation he moved to Atlanta, and within five years he became a vice president with one of the world's largest global-investment firms. Wes leads a large team specializing in investment management for wealthy individuals, families, and large corporations. He is in his sixth year as a financial adviser and one of the

nation's youngest certified financial planner practitioners. He also serves as an instructor at Emory University's prestigious High Net Worth Institute in Atlanta, Georgia.

Kelly *(Carlsbad, California), software executive*

Kelly, 37, earned a B.S. degree in national security and public affairs from the United States Military Academy at West Point. He earned an M.B.A. from the Anderson School at UCLA and a J.D. from the UCLA School of Law simultaneously. After graduating from West Point, Kelly completed Ranger school and served two years as a military intelligence officer in the United States Army. Kelly raised over $5 million in equity financing for three start-up companies, and as the acting president led the sale of one of those start-ups (eteamz.com: the largest amateur-sports portal on the web at the time) for eight figures to a company that has since filed for an IPO. He is the co-founder and chairman of a motor-enthusiast community website called motorpride. com and is currently the president of CoreObjects, an outsourced software development company based in Los Angeles.

Stacy R. *(New York, New York), attorney*

Stacy, 26, is a native New Yorker who received her B.A. in art history from Columbia University, where she graduated with honors. Stacy received her J.D. from Brooklyn Law School, and she currently practices corporate law at a top law firm in New York. Stacy has worked in the legal departments of both Sotheby's Auction House and the Metropolitan Museum of Art in New York. Stacy loves to travel; she has studied abroad in Paris and speaks French. She is an active member of various bar associations and charitable organizations in New York.

Chris *(Long Island, New York), stockbroker*

Chris, 30, was raised in New York, and has been an entrepreneur since he was 11. He started with a candy business, which was followed by a landscaping business by age 14. He sold flowers every holiday, and Christmas trees in the winter. After being a stockbroker for seven years, he opened his own firm. In fewer than five months he was ranked thirteenth in a field of over a thousand brokers, and his branch was eighth out of 171. Perhaps most impressively, Chris has achieved all this with only a high school degree.

John *(San Francisco, California), marketing/real estate director*
John, 24, has lived for the majority of his life in the San Francisco Bay area. He attended the University of California at Berkeley, where he graduated in 2003. While at Cal, John won three division-one national titles in the sport of rugby. After graduation, John submitted a business plan to an automotive magazine, *The Rodder's Journal,* where he was then hired as marketing director. John also co-founded a real-estate-development company in San Francisco, and is currently in the midst of a number of projects. When not at the office, John spends the majority of his free time pursuing his other passion, auto racing.

These are the candidates I met that first day, and I could already tell that it was going to be a fantastic season. Maybe even better than the first.

After saying goodbye to the candidates, I went back to my office to do some business for a couple of hours, and then it was off to NBC studios to shoot the promos for the NBC Primetime Preview 2004/ 2005, known as the Upfronts, coming up next week at Radio City Music Hall. This is a huge, two-hour sales presentation that takes place once a year and generates $2 billion in ad sales. This is Jeff Zucker's forte, and I've learned it's a very important industry event.

I was talking to Craig Plestis, a vice president at NBC, on the way over to the studio, and he mentioned Jeff Zucker's reaction to the first episode he saw of *The Apprentice,* when I was still considered a gamble in their eyes. He said Zucker, who was seeing raw footage without music or any embellishments, became mesmerized by what he was watching and said he knew that it was special right then. By the time he saw the boardroom scene, he knew they had a hit on their hands.

The boardroom was the clincher because it seemed "so real." That's because it *was* real. People don't always understand this, or maybe they forget: I am a businessman, and my instincts are finely honed as a businessman. I can't act my way out of that, ever, and that's what comes across. Jeff Zucker and Mark Burnett recognized this trait in me, and that's why *The Apprentice* has been such a big hit!

The Upfronts would be promoting the second season of *The Apprentice* in a scene set in a small boardroom in an NBC studio. The scene would be a spoof of our boardroom scenes on *The Apprentice,* only we would have five actual NBC executives playing prospective employees. I got to fire them all. George got to slug one, which he did in one take. He didn't need any practice or warm-up shots. Even Sam Solovey, from our first season, did a guest appearance, announcing his big new job at a rival network, which is very good news for *our* network. My secret nickname for him was Sam So-long-now, which is particularly funny to me now, since it seems he's always around—even more so than if I'd hired him. However, I think Sam is enormously talented, and I guarantee that he will be a huge success.

Then, just when I thought my TV day was over—wrong again. We went outside to Rockefeller Plaza to do some shots, and we caused a pedestrian and tour bus jam in the process. I was standing on the back of a truck for everyone to see. How do I get myself into these things? I don't know. But everyone was fast and professional, and we were done in ten minutes. Day One was a wrap. I ducked into my limousine to return to my office and make phone calls.

TUESDAY, MAY 11

The day of the teams' first assignment. We met the film crew and the new eighteen at Toys "R" Us in Times Square. This space is the largest toy store in the world, and it really is incredible. The first assignment always has a certain edge to it, as it marks the true beginning of the show's plot and dynamics. The streets were quiet, since it was 8 A.M., and the store was open just for us. I couldn't help thinking what the new candidates must have been thinking: Last time we started at the New York Stock Exchange on Wall Street, and this time we were at a toy store? But here's a fact: Toys are big business—big to the tune of $20 billion a year. So this was *not* a small-fry assignment.

The group informed me of the two team names and that both the designated leaders are of the opposite sex from the teams they will lead. This could be a good idea, to keep the score a little more balanced than it was the last time, when the women trounced the men for a while. That showed me that maybe they'd learned something from watching the show.

Along with Carolyn, George, and me, several executives from the Mattel toy company—Richard Weintraub, Evelyn Viohl, and Mark Sullivan—were present. They would be in charge of this assignment, which was to develop the prototype for a new commercially viable toy. The target market? A raucous group of children, from six to eight years old. Believe me, that's a tough market.

I told them to get busy and do a good job, and they proceeded to Mattel headquarters in Chelsea to continue their work. I would check on their progress tomorrow. Meanwhile, I returned to the office to get back to work myself.

WEDNESDAY, MAY 12

At 6 P.M., in the midst of an ominous thunderstorm, we drove down to Mattel headquarters for the task resolution. I was looking forward to seeing the results and what the two teams had come up with, even though I prefer grown-up-size toys such as helicopters and airplanes. I remember wishing that we could use my helicopter right then. The traffic was terrible.

We finally arrived in Chelsea, a thriving, bustling area. Mattel occupies a beautiful building with a seven-floor skylit atrium.

As I was descending the stairs into the Mattel conference room, an eight-year-old boy going up the stairs saw me and wasted no time in pointing at me and telling me I was fired, and in no uncertain terms. Fortunately, he was smiling, so it wasn't too scary.

As we waited for the room to be ready for the resolution scene, Richard Devinki, a producer with Mark Burnett's team, mentioned that he had seen *Candide,* an opera by Leonard Bernstein that had recently been revived at Lincoln Center with Patti LuPone. The judge in the opera was dressed to look like me, hair and all, and in one scene he told the exiled Candide, "You're fired!" I couldn't believe I actually made it into an opera, and one by Leonard Bernstein at that. I don't think he'd mind. Bernstein loved New York, too, so I'm in good company.

The eighteen candidates arrived, and Carolyn, George, and I entered the room, which was filled with an amazing assortment of toys. We got right down to business and asked the Mattel executives how the two teams had performed.

They both did well, but it seemed that Apex, the women's team headed by Brad, edged out the men's team. I asked Richard Weintraub of Mattel why he had chosen them, and he said the children in the focus group responded more favorably to their toy. He added that children like action-packed toys, with crashes, energy, and speed—a slam-dunk toy, in other words. The executives also thought their idea had more commercial viability.

I asked him whether there was a chance of ever seeing this new toy in stores, and he said to look for it early next year. It was good enough to develop and market, which is the mark of an effective and imaginative team. It looked like we were off to a fantastic start.

I informed the losing team that I would be seeing them in the boardroom tomorrow, where one of them would be fired. I informed the winning team that the prize for their work would be to have dinner with me in my penthouse apartment that night, along with Melania. Last time, the winning team got to see my apartment and to meet Melania. This time they got to have a filet mignon dinner with us at twilight. I think that's an improvement.

I spent a few minutes talking with Megan Left of Mark Burnett's location crew. While some New York City locations can be a breeze (particularly if I own them), other locations can present an enormous challenge. For example, the shots at the Statue of Liberty required contact with the New York Police Department, the Coast Guard, the U.S. Navy, and Bernadette Castro, the amazing woman who is the commissioner of the New York State Office of Parks, Recreation and Historic Preservation.

Megan told me that finding locations is less of a problem in New York City when I'm involved because they've found that people think I've done a lot for the city and willingly try to be helpful. Several people mentioned to her that *The Apprentice* is like a postcard for NYC. I have to agree.

THURSDAY, MAY 13

The first boardroom scene of the new season took place at 5 P.M. It almost seemed like a reunion to be back there all together again. Aptitude is an interesting thing. I have it for business and making money, and sometimes it's just as clear as day to see when other people don't have it. My first firing wasn't terribly difficult, although I always feel bad for the first person to go because he or she will miss out on so much.

We finished the boardroom scene, and I left immediately to attend a cocktail party for the Metropolitan Golf Association. I went with Carolyn Kepcher and met Rudy Giuliani there. Never a dull moment with Rudy around. We had a great time. The speaker was David Fay of the United States Golf Association, who has done a brilliant job of watching over golf and the game's integrity. He is also a wonderful guy.

FRIDAY, MAY 14

We met in the atrium of Trump Tower at nine in the morning to give the second assignment, which was to create an ice cream flavor and sell it, in tandem with Ciao Bella Gelato. I'm building an ice cream parlor in Trump Tower. Since Starbucks went into the mezzanine level last year, the company now has one of its most lucrative stores anywhere. We are thrilled to have them on the premises.

SATURDAY, MAY 15

At 6 P.M., we met for task resolution in the boardroom. I spent a few minutes talking to Paul Ahern of the art department about what he does, and he described how they covered the mirrors at Petrossian, the restaurant where that night's winning team would indulge in the most expensive caviar in the world. The screen to cover the mirrors is called Hampshire Frost, a translucent plastic that blurs or diffuses any reflection, which is essential for filming there. The details are myriad in shooting a TV series.

It turned out that vanilla was by far the most popular ice cream flavor, and the winning team, Mosaic, capitalized on that consumer preference by coming up with a vanilla-based flavor. This choice, to me, was common sense, and they won because of it. Off they went to Petrossian, and Melania and I went off to Atlantic City for an event at the Taj Mahal.

While being greeted by hundreds of fans waiting outside Trump Tower, I asked them how they liked *The Apprentice*. I was reassured that we would have a strong audience waiting for the new series in the fall.

SUNDAY, MAY 16

A big day for me. My eldest daughter, Ivanka, was graduating from the Wharton School in Philadelphia. She did, as expected, incredibly well. We all went to the ceremony and luncheon at Wharton. It was a beautiful day. On the way back, we stopped at my golf course in Bedminster, New Jersey, and checked things out with Ashley Cooper, who has done an incredible job of making this club such an outstanding success.

We arrived back in New York in time for the second boardroom scene, in which someone from the losing team, Apex, would be fired. This scene was rollicking and very complicated, considering that the teams were doing something as simple as selling ice cream. I couldn't remember a more compelling boardroom scene than this one, even including the firing of Sam and Omarosa.

After being told that the winning team (the men) had dressed for the part in bow ties, I told the losing team that being dressed for the role is an important factor in business. In fact, it's a part of business whether you like it or not. The losing team made no effort to come up with a dress motif that would set them apart. That was just one factor that contributed to their loss, but it was an important one.

We all felt a bit wiped out after this long encounter in the board-room, but there was just enough time to get to Radio City Music Hall for a dress rehearsal for the big Upfront show. I rehearsed the opening with Darrell Hammond, who played me perfectly, as usual, and Jeff Zucker. I got to fire Darrell, but I was hired by Jeff Zucker and NBC, since I'm a "ratings machine." Not a bad transaction. I told Darrell that I had always wanted to play Radio City Music Hall, and from that stage, it truly is a wondrous place.

MONDAY, MAY 17

We had planned to do the third task assignment on the roof of Trump Tower that morning, but as it was foggy out, we would end up doing it in the lobby. The film crews had to reset, so I went up to my office to meet with Bill Rancic, who was reporting for his first day of work. We also had some people from *Dateline* to interview Bill, and Carolyn and George came in for a meeting.

Jim Dowd from NBC arrived, and we discussed the article in *The*

New York Times business section today on the NBC lineup for next fall; Jeff Zucker's promotion to run the entire television entertainment operation of the new media conglomerate, NBC Universal; and the success of *The Apprentice*. The article was comprehensive and well written by Bill Carter, a writer I admire. I may have my tiffs with *The New York Times*, but they've got some terrific people, including Maureen Dowd, Herbert Muschamp, and David Dunlap.

I noticed Jay Bienstock had a new haircut, and he told me that he'll be getting married in two weeks, so by then it would be just the way he likes it to look. Who says men don't plan ahead for important events? I congratulated him on a big decision, and we got to work discussing the task assignment for that day. Jay has already won one Emmy Award, and I suspect there's a lot more to come for him.

I made a call to Ed Molloy, took a call from Regis Philbin, and reviewed a few faxes that came in. Then it was time to go downstairs for the task assignment. We took the elevators to the mezzanine level, surprised a few Starbucks patrons as I walked by, and met Diane Dietz and Matt Barresi, general managers at Procter & Gamble, who would be judges for the outcome of the next task, which was to create and implement a highly visible promotional campaign for a new Crest vanilla mint toothpaste in New York City.

We descended to the lobby on the escalator and greeted the two teams. Each team would work with DeVries Public Relations on its campaign. The team that created the most effective buzz about Crest Vanilla Mint toothpaste, as judged by Procter & Gamble, would win. Each team would have $50,000 in seed money and until the next day at 4 P.M.

I went back up to my office to return calls to Regis Philbin and Phil Riordan of GE. Then I had a meeting with a group from Costas Kondylis's office about furniture for the golf clubhouse in Bedminster, New Jersey. I also had a quick meeting with Allen Weisselberg and Bernie Diamond.

After these meetings, Brian came in to tell me that my limousine was ready, so Melania and I were off to the red-carpet media extravaganza at Radio City for the NBC Upfronts. It took us close to an hour to get into the building because of the media and the crowds. Carolyn, George, and Bill Rancic also received a lot of attention. I saw Sly Stallone, Jeffrey Katzenberg, Matt LeBlanc, and some other friendly faces as we inched our way to the entrance.

Once inside, I was whisked away to my dressing room, where I had five minutes or so to prepare to open the show. Actually, Darrell Hammond opened the show as me, and then I appeared to set things straight. Darrell won me no brownie points by referring to Jeff Zucker as "Jake Zuckerman" and "Jack Zuckerstein," and referring to my hair as "the onion loaf hairstyle," which "I" intend to implement into the dress code when "I" eventually take over NBC.

Then I made my appearance, told Darrell he might have been funny the first few times, that I even enjoyed doing *Saturday Night Live* with him, but that he's just got to go. I had to admit that firing Darrell not only felt good but was a lot of fun. I was relieved when Jeff Zucker appeared onstage to hire *me*. NBC isn't stupid. Jeff then stated that "Jennifer Aniston has better hair than Donald, but Donald has better ratings."

I let Jeff Zucker take over the stage. Watching Jeff in action made me realize that NBC has a true dynamo in residence, the kind of partner I like to have. He noted that twelve of the top twenty shows were unscripted, so reality shows were no passing fancy. He also explained that for twenty years, Thursday nights on NBC have never been surpassed in ratings. In addition, since *The Apprentice* emerged, NBC now has a twenty-eight percent upscale viewer advantage over all other networks. *The Apprentice* was the phenomenon of the season— not only the highest-rated but *the* most upscale show on all of television.

The show continued with an overview of new programs to be

HOW ARISTIDE WAS <u>REALLY</u> DEPOSED:

introduced next season. The lineup included another reality show by Mark Burnett and Jeffrey Katzenberg called *The Contender*, which will star Sylvester Stallone and Sugar Ray Leonard. We also saw previews of another Jeffrey Katzenberg show, *Father of the Pride*, which will feature Siegfried and Roy and their white lions in animated form. We saw a taped interview from Hamburg with both Siegfried and Roy speaking about the new show. Roy has made a partial recovery, and everyone was happy to see him. This interview marked his first public appearance since the accident.

We also saw a preview of *Joey*, Matt LeBlanc's new series; Tom Brokaw appeared; and then Kevin Reilly, the incoming president of NBC Entertainment, closed the show. The Upfronts were intense, and I was impressed with NBC, its lineup, and the terrific presentation. Mark Burnett and I were very pleased with the statistics on *The Apprentice*, and we couldn't help but congratulate each other. Our anticipation for the new season had already been high, and by then it was even higher. Jeff Zucker pulled off a huge event with flying colors, and everyone had a lot of fun. All in all, it was a great afternoon.

But it wasn't over yet. We (meaning several thousand people) went over to Rockefeller Center for a cocktail reception and a photo session, followed by a dinner party for key people.

TUESDAY, MAY 18

We had the task resolution that afternoon for the third assignment, so I could put in close to a full day's work in the office. I returned the many calls I had received the day before, met with Sherman Boxer to go over some advertising campaigns for my properties, and then went over to Trump Park Avenue for a walk-through with John Myers, Phil Riordan, and Don, Jr. I went over my interview commitments, charity events, and review meeting and office updates. Sometimes I feel like I'm in a constant state of catching up, but I'm not complaining. This life's exciting.

I ordered one of those wonderful DT Burgers from the Trump Grill downstairs, and sure enough, Kevin Harris, like clockwork, showed up at my door at the same time as my lunch to brief me on the day's task resolution. He was wearing some kind of shoes that light up when he walks. If he weren't such an effective producer, I'd think he was a space cadet, to use an old but apt term. He ogled my hamburger, so I ordered one for him.

By the time we had finished our lunch, it was time to go down to DeVries Public Relations agency, where the task resolution was to be held. Both Procter & Gamble and DeVries were impressed with the ideas the teams had come up with. That said, the women's team was able to get the Mets' Mike Piazza to brush his teeth in Union Square on behalf of the product. They far outperformed the men's team. But performance isn't everything, and the women were disqualified due to a late budget. The next day's boardroom scene would not be a pleasant one.

WEDNESDAY, MAY 19

That morning I returned to my office to have a meeting with George Ross, where we discussed the events of yesterday's tumultuous task resolution. Minutes and seconds count, whether you're in the Olympics or in business. George mentioned the day's *New York Times* article on my Brazilian partner, Ricardo Bellino, in which Ricardo mentions how I gave him exactly three minutes to sell his idea to me in January 2003. We've been in business together ever since, and he may be bringing *The Apprentice* to Brazil in the near future. He's a good example for these aspiring apprentices of the value of time.

My *Playboy* interview with David Hochman was about to start, followed by a photo shoot. Richard Devinki of Mark Burnett's team stopped by for a minute to brief me on the day's schedule. He wanted to prepare me for the possibility of a long boardroom scene, considering the events of the day before. Richard is in charge of a crew of 275, and he is always calm, unassuming, and professional. I've noticed that Mark Burnett has a knack for finding the best people in the business.

After David Hochman was settled in my office, he began by telling me an interesting fact. In preparing for the interview, he had been given a stack of interviews and articles about me that was several feet high. He was stunned. It was more information than he had for Julia Roberts or Bruce Willis, or anyone else that he has ever interviewed.

We were interrupted a few times during the interview by calls and visits from my staff, but David is a pro and he took it professionally. I enjoyed talking with him. He's informed and easygoing. I told him that an odd thing to me is that it seems my overall image is better since *The Apprentice* started. People see another side of me, and even though I fire people every week on the show, they don't seem to mind. Maybe they can see that I make an effort to be fair. Who knows? It's still a mystery to me. I've always been the same.

After the interview, I ducked down to the fourth floor and met Carolyn and George to prepare for the third boardroom scene. I checked on the crew in the monitor room, and everyone was ready to go. If you've never been behind the scenes of a television show, you'd be surprised at how much goes into it and all the details we as viewers tend to take for granted.

I decided to check out the snack table to see what they had. Production crews have long hours, so nourishment is provided at all times. I don't know what a nutritionist would think of this layout, but it looked healthy enough to me. I even opened the refrigerator, which I was pleased to see was well stocked with Trump Ice water.

Then I spoke with Robin Himmler, from my staff, and asked her how these candidates differed from those from the first season, and she mentioned that they seemed much louder this time around. She could hear a lot of commotion coming from the boardroom. I also noticed that some of the male candidates had put their cards and phone numbers in her prop Rolodex on the set, which was nothing new. It happened last time, too, but she's good-natured and handles the attention well.

Jay Bienstock soon arrived, and we were ready to roll. This boardroom scene could become historic for its histrionics. It was a cross between a soap opera and a court of law. How could something so seemingly simple—a team that went over budget by about ten percent and disqualified itself for being late for a deadline—turn into such chaos?

The scene took a while. After I dismissed the team, except for three of the members, I learned that one of those three had alienated her team to a point where they felt they could not continue to work with her. I had no choice but to find out from the entire team what had actually transpired, so all the dismissed women were called back into the boardroom immediately.

We spent a lot of time talking about the events that were bothering the women and whether or not this person should be given another chance. Given the unanimous feelings of the rest of the team, I saw that I had to act decisively for the good of the show. The decision was serious and important. And difficult, but she had to go.

Afterward, Mark Burnett, Craig Plestis, and I discussed the intensity and length of the last two boardroom scenes, each of which had taken close to two hours. They were riveting to shoot, and the monitor room thought they were great television, so we decided there could be a Saturday-night episode that would feature the boardroom scene in its entirety. We left the set after a long night and set a meeting to discuss this idea further.

THURSDAY, MAY 20

At 9 A.M. I went downstairs to meet the Mark Burnett crew; we were going to meet the candidates at Jean Georges, the restaurant in the

Trump International Hotel and Tower, for the fourth task assignment. It was a perfect spring day in New York. We traveled over to the West Side and saw the seemingly never-ending construction at Columbus Circle. I'm not the only one who thinks the construction is endless: Regis did a comedy segment on his show about how this entire area had been in scaffolding and under demolition and construction for so long that when the scaffolding finally came down, people couldn't figure out what was different about their neighborhood, though they knew something was.

It has looked like a disaster zone for years. The traffic jams have been unbelievable, too, and we're talking years, not months. It's getting there, but it's been an ordeal for everyone. Fortunately, the Trump International Hotel & Tower has been spared this mess by its location, which is directly across from Central Park on Central Park itself, not on Broadway and Columbus Circle, like the Time Warner building. I still wonder whether the new tenants there are enjoying their view of my building. Location isn't always the most important consideration, but in instances like this, it can be.

Mark Burnett and I greeted Jean-Georges inside his restaurant as the apprentice candidates entered the formal dining room to await their next task assignment. This room is beautifully serene—so much so that everyone seemed uncharacteristically calm. Someone mentioned that the room is very much like a Milton Avery painting, which we agreed was a good observation.

Bill Rancic was also with us today. We decided it was fitting, the return of the original apprentice to the second season of the show. Bill mentioned that he cannot walk down the streets in Chicago without being mobbed. He is a big celebrity there, as it's his hometown. Apparently he has also been named the most eligible bachelor of the year. If any of this attention has gone to his head, we've seen no indication of it whatsoever.

Carolyn, Bill, and I entered the dining room, and I explained that since George Ross was away on business, Bill would be replacing him for this week. I also explained that they were standing in the highest-rated restaurant in New York City, which also happens to be in the highest-rated hotel. I also told them that Tim Zagat is a friend of mine, a great guy as well as a talented one, and his Zagat guides to restaurants are considered the bibles in the restaurant business. The name is just that powerful.

The Zagat guides include ratings by customers, and the editors compile all the information they receive, in addition to their own scouting, to come up with fair and insightful reviews that combine comments on food, service, decor, and ambiance. It's updated every year, so restaurants stay on top of their game.

Then we got to their task. We had two empty spaces that were to be made into restaurants. If the two teams couldn't decide who got which space, they would flip a coin. By the next night they would have to be serving food and bringing customers in from the street. In addition, someone from Zagat would be there, incognito, to review their work. I wished them well and gave the floor to Carolyn and Bill.

Both Carolyn and Bill mentioned that the two teams look "too well rested," and Bill informed them that it would only get worse from there on out—especially with this particular task assignment. Anyone who thinks running a restaurant looks like fun hasn't ever been in the restaurant business. The margin of failure is wide.

I went back into the front dining room and talked with Jean-Georges and Mark for a while. The other breakfast customers had adjusted to us by then and just carried on with their newspapers and conversations. It's amazing how quickly New Yorkers can adapt to anything. I headed back to my office.

A bit later, Kevin Harris arrived to take us out to my jet at La Guardia Airport for an inside shoot. When we arrived, it was hard not to miss it, with "TRUMP" printed on it in twenty-four-carat gold. Twenty-four-carat gold cannot be duplicated. It looks great, and if you're ever at La Guardia, be sure to keep an eye out for it—you can't miss it.

My pilot, Mike Donovan, greeted us, even though we wouldn't be flying anywhere that day. We went inside the aircraft to film a few scenes and shots, and while we waited for everyone to set up, Mike and I reminisced about the first time we met, ten years ago. He gave me permission to tell this story, in case it helps those people who have interview nerves.

Ten years ago, when I was looking to hire a pilot, Mike was invited to my office in Trump Tower to meet me. He bought a new suit, stopped at St. Patrick's Cathedral for good graces, and showed up at my office. We had been chatting a bit when suddenly Mike somersaulted off his chair and onto the floor. He just fell off his chair and disappeared from view. That made quite an impression; in fact, no one before or since has topped that performance. But Mike was sure that was the last time he'd ever see me. Needless to say, he was wrong. He was the right guy—just a little nervous. He's kept my jet on balance for ten straight years.

Once the crew had set up, we did a few takes in the jet. It didn't take too long, but it was about eighty degrees out that day and we had to turn off the air-conditioning because of the noise level. Additionally, every time another jet took off or landed, we had to stop and wait for the noise to subside. We finally finished and did a few shots outside. Then it was back into the limousine.

I was accompanied by Matthew John, the director of photography, who was nominated for an Emmy for his camera work the first season. He's been with Mark Burnett for eight years and is a quiet and professional guy. I asked him which was easier, the first season of *The Apprentice* or this time around. He said the first show was easier in the sense that we had a certain anonymity that's not possible now. On the other hand, we can perform bigger tasks, since we are a proven entity. Trying to carry things out incognito is not as easy now, because people know the show to be a hit. But we have the biggest companies wanting to be a part of it, whereas before it was a risk for them. Matthew also explained that there was a minimum of fourteen camera crews working a twenty-four-hour staggered schedule every day for forty-six days to cover the action involved with the show.

I asked him about the inevitable spin-offs and mentioned that I'd seen Richard Branson on television talking about his show. I like Richard Branson a lot, and his show looks interesting and not too similar. Then we got on the subject of Mark Cuban. I have to say that right after he lost in the play-offs, I felt bad for him. But nobody's going to beat *The Apprentice*.

Before long, we were back at Trump Tower, and I told Matthew I was sure to see him again soon. There was a crowd in front of Trump Tower, so I ducked out of the limousine and made a run for it to the door.

FRIDAY, MAY 21

Believe it or not, I had a day off from *The Apprentice*. This time off would be a rare occasion in our forty-six-day shoot schedule. In the morning I gave the commencement address at Wagner College on Staten Island and received an honorary doctorate.

I told the graduates that they already have what it takes to succeed. They have achieved, and they've been given, the tools necessary for success. All they have to do is apply themselves one hundred percent every single day to their endeavors and remain tenacious until they're 102 years old, if necessary. There's something exciting about graduations, and I enjoyed this one in particular.

After tending to some business in my office, I prepared myself to introduce Jessica Simpson at Madison Square Garden later that night. It was a pleasure. Melania accompanied me.

SATURDAY, MAY 22

We had a 9 A.M. call in Trump Tower for the resolution of the restaurant assignment. I took the elevator down and met Carolyn Kepcher and Bill Rancic. We were looking forward to seeing what had been accomplished by the two teams.

The women's team earned a combined Zagat rating of fifty-seven, while the men received a rating of sixty-one. They were rated in three categories: food, decor, and service. The descriptive portion of the ratings said the women appeared to be "uptight stewardesses," while the men were "hot eye-candy waiters," plus they scored higher in decor and service than the women. For once it appears that the men beat out the women in sex appeal, and once again the men's team won. Their prize was a great one: They would get to go over to Rudy Giuliani's new office at Times Square and have a discussion with the man himself.

Ducking the crowds outside of Trump Tower proved to be another highlight of a busy morning, but we were beginning to get used to it. I even rolled down my window and waved. Noel, my driver, is all business, however, and he cut the episode short. We took off down Fifth Avenue.

After the article came out describing me as the Elvis of Business, my security team took to saying "Elvis is leaving the building" whenever I was on my way out. I was sure Noel was behind that, so I asked him to put the word out to stop those announcements. They did. Now they say "Mr. Trump is leaving the building" instead.

We arrived at Rudy's offices high above Times Square, an area that is now thriving due to Rudy's vigilance and foresight, and we were met by Rudy and his lovely wife, Judith. I made a brief introduction and then left the rest to Rudy. True to form, he generously gave over an hour of his undivided attention to the candidates and their questions, and then gave them a tour of the mementos in his office, such as the Wilkinson sword given to him by Queen Elizabeth II when he was knighted, and a painting of St. Paul's Chapel, near the World Trade Center, which served as a refuge for the rescue workers and remained miraculously unscathed during the terrorist attack in 2001.

After hearing about the candidates' restaurant assignment, Rudy told them that the toughest job he's ever had was being a waiter; that as a young man, he had wanted to be either a priest or a doctor; that he was initially a poor public speaker, which he finally remedied by backing away from the podium and his notes and just talking to the audience; that he sees business leadership and political leadership as being the same; that he has a sign on his desk that reads "I'm Responsible"; and that he thinks leaders are made, not born, but, of course, you have to be born first.

His advice to the candidates was to find a good role model, a great example in life. For him, Joe DiMaggio was one, because he led by example. So was Winston Churchill, whom he used as a model when he was a student and also when he was mayor, for the simple reason that Churchill knew how to focus and would concentrate on the *solution* of a problem rather than the problem itself. Rudy also believes you can train yourself to be an optimist.

Pamela asked about women leaders he has admired, and Rudy mentioned Margaret Thatcher and Golda Meir. He also advised the group to find out what's really important to them first, to know their own core, and to get on top of every day before it gets on top of them. Being mayor of New York City taught him that one. If one inch of snow fell, he would receive calls because the plows weren't out yet. You can't plow one inch of snow, but don't try to tell New Yorkers that.

After the discussion, all the candidates asked him questions, and he signed books for them and walked them to the elevator. What a memorable morning they had with one of the great men of our time. We thank Rudy for that.

We had a break until 6 P.M., so I decided to drive up to Trump National Golf Club in Briarcliff Manor to check things out and get in a round of golf. It was a humid day, but the course was looking lush and inviting. I love having my own golf courses to play on.

By 6 P.M. we were back for the boardroom scene, featuring the women's team, who lost in the Zagat rating. Bill, Carolyn, and I talked about our afternoon, and then it was back to business as usual. Funny how doing a television show about business has actually become business to us.

I began by mentioning how Rudy Giuliani spoke about leadership to the men's team, and how that seems to be lacking among the women. Even the women admitted the men's team exhibited solidarity and camaraderie lacking among themselves. This particular boardroom scene was an easy call because the leader did not display leadership qualities, and she refused to call into the boardroom the person who had lost $2,000 for the team. A bad call on her part, and even Carolyn had to say that this group of women made her embarrassed as a businesswoman. During the boardroom scene, I remember thinking that I hoped they could pull it together, and soon.

We were finished by 8 P.M., and Melania was making dinner tonight, so we headed upstairs for a relaxing evening at home. Tomorrow, after the task assignment, I would be the grand marshal in the Salute to Israel Parade on Fifth Avenue, so it would be a busy and exciting day. I would be walking in the parade with Howard Lorber and the New York Board of Rabbis. I've always enjoyed parades, and this parade would be a special one.

I have to sign off on *The Apprentice* coverage now, as I don't want to ruin the show by giving you too much information prior to airing. I hope you've enjoyed the background information, and I hope you will tune in and watch for yourself these amazing episodes. As much as I like to write, I can't imagine writing a script for drama like this. Just seeing it unfold every day is as surprising as it is entertaining, and I hope I've given you an idea of what it's like behind the scenes. Enjoy the show, and stay tuned. I can guarantee you'll learn a few things.

Acknowledgments

Like my previous book, *How to Get Rich,* this book never would have happened without the hard work and help of Meredith McIver. Also, Norma Foerderer, who manages my schedule, kept this project on schedule.

Thanks to the people at Random House, particularly editor Ben Loehnen, who did a terrific job under deadline pressure and has the mind of a first-rate capitalist; editor in chief Jonathan Karp and publisher Gina Centrello, who made sure Random House paid me an even bigger fortune for this book and provided valuable editorial direction; associate publishers Anthony Ziccardi and Elizabeth McGuire; executive director of publicity Carol Schneider; director of publicity Thomas Perry; associate director of publicity Elizabeth Fogarty; associate editor Jonathan Jao; art director Gene Mydlowski; managing editor Benjamin Dreyer; production chief Lisa Feuer; design director Carole Lowenstein; production manager Richard Elman; production editor Janet Wygal; copy editor Ginny Carroll; advertising director Magee Finn; rights directors Claire Tisne and Rachel Bernstein; and everyone in the Random House sales force, which remains the best in the business. Special thanks to Donald M. Karp, of Independence Community Bank, and Sean Compton, of Clear Channel.

At the Trump Organization, I am surrounded by professionals: Matthew Calamari, Allen Weisselberg, George Ross, Bernie Diamond, Jason Greenblatt, Rhona Graff, Tony Morace, Andy Weiss, Don, Jr., Jeff, Eric, Robin, and many more.

Meredith McIver would like to thank Richard Casares, Steve Palitz, Tassos of Patmos, Chris Papanikolas, her family, Mark Burnett's team, and the members of the Trump Organization, especially Rhona Graff, Robin Himmler, and Renee St. Jean. A very special thank-you to Norma Foerderer for her generosity, to Melania Knauss for her kind assistance, and, as always, to Donald Trump for being himself.

Behind the Scenes
at The Trump Organization

Index

Wright, Suzanne, 169, 195
Wynn, Steve, 101, 137, 179,
191

Zagat, Tim, 223
Zagat guides, 223, 226, 228
Zucker, Jeff
    comment about *The Apprentice*
        as comedy by, 169
    and final episode of *the*
        Apprentice, xxiii, 195

New York Times article about,
    215
and ratings for *The Apprentice*,
    161, 178
reaction to first episode of *The*
    Apprentice by, 208–9
and Trump as savior of NBC,
    136
and Trump's appearance on
    Saturday Night Live, 149,
    152, 154
and Upfronts, 214, 216, 218

DONALD J. TRUMP is the very definition of the American success story, continually setting standards of excellence while expanding his interests in real estate, gaming, sports, and entertainment. In 2003, he partnered with NBC and executive producer Mark Burnett on *The Apprentice,* which became a smash hit, the highest-rated debut of the season, and finished number one. In 2004, the partnership returned for another two seasons of the hit show and received four Emmy nominations. He and NBC are also partners in the ownership and broadcast rights for the three largest beauty competitions in the world.

In New York City, the Trump signature is synonymous with the most prestigious addresses, including the renowned Trump Tower, Trump International Hotel & Tower, Trump Park Avenue, Trump World Tower, and the seventeen-building Trump Place on Riverside Boulevard. In the gaming arena, the Trump Organization is one of the world's largest operators of hotels and casinos, most notably in Atlantic City, New Jersey, as well as Trump National Golf Club in Briarcliff Manor, New York, and other great courses throughout the United States.

Trump is the number one *New York Times* bestselling author of *How to Get Rich, The Art of the Deal, Surviving at the Top,* and *The Art of the Comeback,* as well as *The America We Deserve.* All told, these books have sold millions of copies.

An ardent philanthropist, Trump is involved with numerous civic and charitable organizations. In June 2000, he received his greatest honor, the Hotel and Real Estate Visionary of the Century award, given by the UJA Federation.

For more information on Donald Trump and the Trump Organization, visit www.trumponline.com.

MEREDITH MCIVER was a Ford Foundation scholar and is a graduate of the University of Utah. She lives on the Upper West Side of Manhattan and is a member of the Trump Organization.

ABOUT THE TYPE

This book was set in Galliard, a typeface designed by Matthew Carter for the Mergenthaler Linotype Company in 1978. Galliard is based on the sixteenth-century typefaces of Robert Granjon.